# SpringerBriefs in Law

SpringerBriefs present concise summaries of cutting-edge research and practical applications across a wide spectrum of fields. Featuring compact volumes of 50 to 125 pages, the series covers a range of content from professional to academic. Typical topics might include:

- A timely report of state-of-the art analytical techniques
- A bridge between new research results, as published in journal articles, and a contextual literature review
- A snapshot of a hot or emerging topic
- A presentation of core concepts that students must understand in order to make independent contributions

SpringerBriefs in Law showcase emerging theory, empirical research, and practical application in Law from a global author community. SpringerBriefs are characterized by fast, global electronic dissemination, standard publishing contracts, standardized manuscript preparation and formatting guidelines, and expedited production schedules.

Dennis Hirsch · Timothy Bartley ·
Aravind Chandrasekaran · Davon Norris ·
Srinivasan Parthasarathy · Piers Norris Turner

# Business Data Ethics

Emerging Models for Governing AI
and Advanced Analytics

Dennis Hirsch  
Moritz College of Law and Department of Computer Science and Engineering, The Ohio State University  
Columbus, OH, USA

Aravind Chandrasekaran  
Fisher College of Business  
The Ohio State University  
Columbus, OH, USA

Srinivasan Parthasarathy  
Department of Computer Science and Engineering  
The Ohio State University  
Columbus, OH, USA

Timothy Bartley  
Earth Commons Institute and Department of Sociology,  
Georgetown University  
Washington, D.C., USA

Davon Norris  
Organizational Studies Program  
University of Michigan  
Ann Arbor, MI, USA

Piers Norris Turner  
Department of Philosophy  
Center for Ethics and Human Values  
The Ohio State University  
Columbus, OH, USA

ISSN 2192-855X    ISSN 2192-8568 (electronic)  
SpringerBriefs in Law  
ISBN 978-3-031-21490-5    ISBN 978-3-031-21491-2 (eBook)  
https://doi.org/10.1007/978-3-031-21491-2

This open-access book was funded by the Ohio State University Program on Data and Governance, a program of the OSU Moritz College of Law and OSU Translational Data Analytics Institute.

© The Editor(s) (if applicable) and The Author(s) 2024. This book is an open access publication.

**Open Access** This book is licensed under the terms of the Creative Commons Attribution 4.0 International License (http://creativecommons.org/licenses/by/4.0/), which permits use, sharing, adaptation, distribution and reproduction in any medium or format, as long as you give appropriate credit to the original author(s) and the source, provide a link to the Creative Commons license and indicate if changes were made.

The images or other third party material in this book are included in the book's Creative Commons license, unless indicated otherwise in a credit line to the material. If material is not included in the book's Creative Commons license and your intended use is not permitted by statutory regulation or exceeds the permitted use, you will need to obtain permission directly from the copyright holder.

The use of general descriptive names, registered names, trademarks, service marks, etc. in this publication does not imply, even in the absence of a specific statement, that such names are exempt from the relevant protective laws and regulations and therefore free for general use.

The publisher, the authors, and the editors are safe to assume that the advice and information in this book are believed to be true and accurate at the date of publication. Neither the publisher nor the authors or the editors give a warranty, expressed or implied, with respect to the material contained herein or for any errors or omissions that may have been made. The publisher remains neutral with regard to jurisdictional claims in published maps and institutional affiliations.

This Springer imprint is published by the registered company Springer Nature Switzerland AG  
The registered company address is: Gewerbestrasse 11, 6330 Cham, Switzerland

Paper in this product is recyclable.

*To our families, with gratitude for their support.*

*Timothy Bartley*
*Aravind Chandrasekaran*
*Dennis Hirsch*
*Davon Norris*
*Srinivasan Parthasarathy*
*Piers Norris Turner*

# Preface

As this book goes to print, the rapid emergence of large language models such as ChatGPT has brought the governance of AI and advanced analytics to the top of the news cycle and made it a subject of intense interest in legislatures and boardrooms across the nation. Along with their many productive aspects, large language models such as ChatGPT can result in harmful bias, privacy invasion, inequality, labor displacement, misinformation, hate speech, manipulation, loss of intellectual property, fraud, and other injuries. The CEO of OpenAI, the company that created ChatGPT, has warned that these models could even cause the "extinction" of humanity. These warnings have, unsurprisingly, driven calls for governments to regulate large language models and for the companies that develop and deploy them to do so ethically, safely, and responsibly. The pressing need to govern AI has emerged in recent months as one of the key issues of the day, though some despair as to whether it is even possible.

The issue is hardly new, however. Private and public sector organizations have been integrating AI and advanced analytics into their operations and products for years. Scholars, journalists, policymakers, and others have long warned of AI's and advanced analytics' threats to fairness, equity, privacy, and accountability. Efforts to mitigate these threats have been underway for some time. The field of AI governance need not start from scratch with the release of ChatGPT. There is a foundation on which to build.

This book describes part of that foundation. Between 2017 and 2019, the authors interviewed and surveyed dozens of professionals at the cutting edge of private sector data and AI ethics management, and the consultants and think tanks that advise them. These ethics managers told us about their fears, their motivations, and, most importantly, their strategies for spotting and addressing the risks that their companies' use of AI and advanced analytics could create. At the time of our research, governments were only just beginning to engage with these threats. But certain companies—for reasons that we will discuss below and that largely spring from their own strategic interests—were already beginning to identify and take measures to address them. We wanted to understand what they were doing, and why they were doing it.

We knew that, to make sense of what we were seeing, we would need interdisciplinary expertise. We accordingly built a research team that included scholars of business management, computer science, law, philosophy, and sociology. The sharing of our different, and sometimes quite divergent, perspectives on what we were seeing allowed each of us to understand more than we would have on our own. We bring that convergent perspective to this book.

This book describes private sector ethics managers' accounts of the threats that their own companies' uses of AI and advanced analytics could create; why their organizations sought to address these threats, even when the law did not require them to do so; and, most of all, how their organization sought to spot and reduce such threats, including the very real limits of and gaps in these efforts. It provides a snapshot of the emergence of the field of data and AI ethics management.

The governance of advanced analytics and AI has continued to evolve since the time of our research. But the core questions about whether to go beyond legal minimums, and how an organization should think about and act on its ethical responsibilities, will be with us for many years to come. Our work shows this emerging field of management practice at a formative point and so reveals the foundations on which today's AI governance is being built. It should be useful to organizations seeking to establish their own data and AI ethics management programs, legislators and policymakers working to shape AI governance, and members of the public who are wondering whether such governance is possible and, if it is, what form it should take.

It should also be of interest to our fellow scholars of self-regulation and business data ethics. Like us, they think about why companies engage in self-regulation, what self-regulation can accomplish, and where government regulation is needed. To date, much of this work has focused on the environmental, labor, and worker safety areas. This book helps to expand the field to encompass AI and the algorithmic economy. We hope that it stimulates more interest in, and study of, this growing area of business governance practice.

The law and policy of advanced analytics and AI is coming. In the years, since we completed our research, legislators, and policymakers have proposed, and in some cases passed, laws specifically designed to regulate and tame business use of these technologies. Among other things, this emerging legal framework requires companies to undertake management practices such as impact assessments, audits, or stakeholder engagement. That is a positive development and one to which we hope this book contributes. But the necessarily limited nature of such regulations in a complex and fast-changing landscape means that law, while critical, is rarely sufficient. Law depends on, and seeks to motivate, responsible governance by regulated parties themselves. Going forward, data ethics management will continue to play an important role in aligning advanced analytics and AI with social values.

| | |
|---|---:|
| Columbus, USA | Dennis Hirsch |
| Washington, D.C., USA | Timothy Bartley |
| Columbus, USA | Aravind Chandrasekaran |
| Ann Arbor, USA | Davon Norris |
| Columbus, USA | Srinivasan Parthasarathy |
| Columbus, USA | Piers Norris Turner |
| August 2023 | |

# Acknowledgements

This research was supported by The Ohio State University Program on Data and Governance, a grant from the Risk Institute at The Ohio State University Fisher College of Business, and a gift from Facebook (now Meta). It would not have been possible without the ongoing support of The Ohio State University Moritz College of Law, Department of Computer Science and Engineering, and Translational Data Analytics Institute (TDAI). The authors appreciate the assistance of the Centre for Information Policy Leadership (CIPL), the Computer and Communications Industry Association (CCIA), the Future of Privacy Forum (FPF), the Information Accountability Foundation (IAF), and the Software and Information Industry Association (SIIA), each of which distributed the survey to its members. Special thanks to Christina Drummond, Gillian Thomson, and Abby Norris Turner for their assistance with this project and to the Privacy Law Scholars Conference for giving us an opportunity to present an early draft of this work.

# Contents

| | | |
|---|---|---|
| 1 | **Introduction** | 1 |
| | References | 8 |
| 2 | **Studying Data Ethics Management: Research Methodology** | 11 |
| | 2.1 Interviews | 12 |
| | 2.2 Survey | 13 |
| | References | 16 |
| 3 | **Risks: From Privacy and Manipulation to Bias and Displacement** | 17 |
| | 3.1 Privacy Violations | 19 |
| | 3.2 Manipulation | 20 |
| | 3.3 Bias Against Protected Classes | 21 |
| | 3.4 Increased Power Imbalances | 23 |
| | 3.5 Error | 23 |
| | 3.6 Opacity and Procedural Unfairness | 23 |
| | 3.7 Displacement of Labor | 24 |
| | 3.8 Pressure to Conform | 24 |
| | 3.9 Intentional, Harmful Use of Analytics | 25 |
| | References | 26 |
| 4 | **What is Business Data Ethics Management?** | 27 |
| 5 | **Motivations—Why Do Companies Pursue Data Ethics?** | 33 |
| | 5.1 Build Reputation and Sustain Trust | 34 |
| | 5.2 Anticipate Emerging Regulation | 38 |
| | 5.3 Recruit and Retain Employees | 41 |
| | 5.4 Make Faster and Better Risk-Based Decisions | 42 |
| | 5.5 Achieve Competitive Advantage | 43 |
| | 5.6 Fulfill Corporate Values | 44 |
| | References | 44 |

| 6 | **Drawing Substantive Lines** | 47 |
|---|---|---|
| | 6.1 Published Data Ethics Principles | 49 |
| | 6.2 Informal Standards | 52 |
| | 6.3 Risk Management Frameworks | 55 |
| | 6.4 Formal Principles in Action | 56 |
| | 6.5 Policy: The Missing Middle Layer | 58 |
| | References | 60 |
| 7 | **Management Structures and Functions** | 61 |
| | 7.1 Organizational Structures | 62 |
| |     7.1.1 Privacy Office | 63 |
| |     7.1.2 Legal Department | 63 |
| |     7.1.3 The Chief Data Ethics Officer | 64 |
| |     7.1.4 The Data Ethics Committee | 65 |
| |     7.1.5 Philosophers in the Corporate Ranks | 66 |
| |     7.1.6 From Compliance to Strategy | 66 |
| 8 | **Management Processes** | 69 |
| | 8.1 Processes for Spotting Data Ethics Issues | 70 |
| |     8.1.1 Touring the Business Units | 71 |
| |     8.1.2 Hub and Spokes | 71 |
| | 8.2 Processes for Deciding Data Ethics Issues | 76 |
| |     8.2.1 Just in Time Data Ethics | 76 |
| | 8.3 Broader Themes | 78 |
| |     8.3.1 Streamlined Versus Deliberative | 78 |
| |     8.3.2 Internal Versus System-Wide Focus | 79 |
| | References | 81 |
| 9 | **Technical Solutions** | 83 |
| | 9.1 Data Privacy and Anonymization | 84 |
| | 9.2 Algorithmic Fairness | 86 |
| | 9.3 The Clear and Pressing Need for Explainable Algorithms | 87 |
| | 9.4 Algorithmic Auditing of Data Use | 88 |
| | 9.5 Systems Technologies to Enable Governance | 88 |
| | References | 89 |
| 10 | **Data Analytics for the Social Good** | 93 |
| | References | 97 |
| 11 | **Conclusion** | 99 |

# About the Authors

**Dennis Hirsch** is Professor of Law and of Computer Science at The Ohio State University where he also serves as Director of the Program on Data and Governance and as a core faculty member of the Translational Data Analytics Institute (TDAI). His research and teaching, and the program that he directs, focus on the law, policy, ethics, and management of advanced analytics and AI. The author of numerous articles and an award-winning book, he is the co-editor of the SSRN *eJournal on Artificial Intelligence—Law, Policy, and Ethics*, the founding Chair of TDAI's Responsible Data Science Community of Practice, the founder of the Ohio Data Ethics Working Group, a member of the Advisory Board for the International Association of Privacy Professionals' (IAPP) AI Governance Center, and a member of the Organization for Economic Cooperation and Development's (OECD) Expert Group on AI Risk and Accountability. In 2010, he served as a Fulbright Senior Professor at the University of Amsterdam where he studied Dutch privacy regulation. He received his J.D. from Yale Law School.

**Timothy Bartley** is a Professor in the Earth Commons Institute and Department of Sociology at Georgetown University. He previously held positions at Washington University in St. Louis, Stockholm University, Ohio State University, and Indiana University. He is an organizational, political, and economic sociologist, whose research focuses largely on private forms of regulation and questions of fairness and sustainability in global industries. His previous work includes the book *Rules without Rights: Land, Labor, and Private Authority in the Global Economy* (Oxford University Press, 2018) and articles such as "Global Markets, Corporate Assurances, and the Legitimacy of State Intervention" (*American Sociological Review*, 2022), "Transnational Corporations and Global Governance" (*Annual Review of Sociology*, 2018), "Shaming the Corporation" (*American Sociological Review*, 2014), and "The Digital Surveillance Society" (*Contemporary Sociology*, 2019). He received his Ph.D. from the University of Arizona and has been lucky to spend time as a visiting scholar at the University of Konstanz, University of St. Gallen, Max Planck Institute for the Study of Societies, MIT, Princeton, and Sun Yat-sen University.

**Aravind Chandrasekaran** is the Fisher Distinguished Professor in Operations and Business Analytics at the Fisher College of Business, The Ohio State University. He received his Ph.D. in Operations and Management Sciences from the University of Minnesota. His research investigates innovation, learning, and knowledge creation issues in a variety of industries including high-tech R&D, manufacturing, and health care. His research has been published in all top OM journals. He currently serves as the Associate Dean for Graduate Programs and Executive Education at the Fisher College of Business. He oversees all the graduate programs including full-time MBA, working professional MBA, specialized master's as well as executive master's programs including EMBA, the Master of Business in Operational Excellence (MBOE), and non-degree executive education. He has developed several custom teaching and research programs for organizations such as Tata Consultancy Services (TCS), Ford Motor Company, and Zimmer. He has won several teaching awards including the 2016 and 2012 Best Outstanding Core Professor Award (WPMBA), as well as the 2013 Pace Setter Award for Teaching Excellence.

**Davon Norris** is Assistant Professor of Organizational Studies at the University of Michigan, is an economic sociologist who tries to understand how our tools for determining what is valuable, worthwhile, or good are implicated in patterns of inequality with an acute concern for racial inequality. Generally, this empirically manifests in work that studies credit, debt, and finance. However, he more specifically investigates the functioning and consequences of a range of scores or ratings, from state and municipal government credit ratings to algorithmic consumer credit scores. By centering questions of valuation, his research speaks across an array of disciplines and brings into relief normative questions about the nature and possibility of ameliorating (racial) inequality and nurturing economic justice in the contemporary USA. His research has been published in outlets such as Social Forces, Socio-Economic Review, Social Problems, and Sociological Forum and has received awards from the Future of Privacy Forum and American Sociological Association. He is a three-time Buckeye receiving his BS in Accounting (2014), his MA in Sociology (2018), and his Ph.D. (2022) in Sociology all from The Ohio State University.

**Srinivasan Parthasarathy** received his Ph.D. in Computer Science from the University of Rochester, New York, USA. He is a Professor in the Computer Science and Engineering Department at the Ohio State University (OSU). He directs the data mining research laboratory at OSU and co-directs the university-wide undergraduate program in Data analytics as well as the Community of Practice in Responsible Data Science. His research interests are broadly in the areas of data mining, machine learning, databases, and bioinformatics. He is a recipient of an Ameritech Faculty fellowship in 2001, an NSF CAREER award in 2003, a DOE Early Career Award in 2004, and multiple grants or fellowships from IBM, Google, and Microsoft. His papers have received fifteen best paper awards or similar honors (best of conference selection), and many of his works have transitioned to practice, ranging from commercial implementations to widespread use in clinical practice for disease diagnosis. He is a frequent distinguished and keynote speaker at various conferences and recently completed his final term as chair (elected) of the steering committee for the SIAM data mining conference series. He is a fellow of the Institute of Electrical and Electronics Engineers (IEEE) for contributions to high-performance data mining and network science, a fellow of the Asia-Pacific AI Association for contributions to scalable data mining and graph representation learning, and a Distinguished Fellow at the Robert Bosch Center of Data Science and AI for his work in data science and AI.

**Piers Norris Turner** is Associate Professor of Philosophy and Director of the Center for Ethics and Human Values at Ohio State University. His research on utilitarianism and liberal political thought, especially in the moral and political philosophy of John Stuart Mill, has appeared in leading journals including *Ethics, Utilitas,* and the *Journal of the History of Philosophy*. He has co-edited *Public Reason in Political Philosophy: Classic Sources and Contemporary Commentaries* (Routledge) and a collection of unpublished writings by Karl Popper called *After The Open Society* (Routledge). Currently, he is working on a manuscript entitled Mill's Ethics (CUP).

# Chapter 1
# Introduction

**Key Take-Aways**

- This book conveys the findings from an empirical study, conducted between 2017 and 2019, of how and why businesses seek to manage the threats and ethical challenges that their own use of data, advanced analytics and AI can create.
- The research sought to explore three core questions: (1) How do business organizations at the forefront of data ethics management conceptualize the threats that their use of data, advanced analytics and AI create for others, and the ethical challenges that this poses for the organization itself? (2) If it is true that the law does not yet require businesses to reduce these threats, then why are certain companies pursuing this end? (3) How are businesses pursuing data ethics management? Which substantive benchmarks, management structures, processes, and technical solutions do they employ to ground and operationalize their ethical responsibilities as they conceive them?
- Much of the scholarly literature on data ethics focuses on normative analysis of data ethics principles and of regulatory frameworks. Empirical work on data ethics management can inform regulation and complement high-level data ethics principles, but scholars have done far less of this type of work. This book helps to fill that gap.
- The researchers used a "grounded theory" approach that moves iteratively between observation and theory to identify the best conceptual framework for understanding the observed realities. This study concludes that research on "beyond compliance" behavior and the "social license to operate" best fits the behavior that businesses refer to as data ethics management.
- To date, scholarly work on the social license to operate has focused largely on environmental management, working conditions, and human rights in global

> supply chains. This book suggests that, in today's digital and algorithmic economy, the "social license to operate" is coming increasingly to depend as well on an organization's data ethics performance.

Some years ago, an issuer of subprime credit cards (cards issued to people who generally do not qualify for them) sought to identify which of its current customers were most likely to default on their credit card bills and then to cut their credit limits in half (FTC v. CompuCredit 2008). The company used a "behavioral scoring model" for this purpose. It first pulled together data on which of its *past* customers had defaulted. It then looked for a pattern: did these defaulting customers tend to use their cards in ways that their non-defaulting peers did not? The company found such a pattern. Defaulting card holders had used their cards at pawn shops, massage parlors, and marital counselors far more frequently than their non-defaulting peers.[1] Based on this correlation, the company predicted that current card holders who use their cards to pay for these particular items presented a high risk of default and proceeded to cut their credit limits in half—an action that, in and of itself, did not violate the law.[2]

Should the company have done this? Even if it is legal, is it *right* to reduce someone's credit line by half because they have used their card to pay for marital counseling services? Is it more (or less) justifiable to reduce it because the person used the card at a pawn shop or massage parlor? One can easily come up with arguments on each side of this question. On the one hand, some might point out that reducing default rates will strengthen the company's bottom line and so enable it to issue more credit cards, at lower interest rates, to those who would otherwise not be eligible for credit. These proponents might also explain that this practice prevents vulnerable card holders from getting over-extended and so saves them from the emotional pain and lasting economic damage that a default can cause.

On the other hand, critics of the company's action might decry the unfairness of penalizing those whose only sin is to try to preserve or improve their marriage. They could further point out that those who use a card for marital counseling and then see their credit line cut in half will be less likely to seek out marital counseling in the future. That could hurt not only the card holders themselves but also their spouses, children, and society at large. These critics could also ask whether people of one race, gender, or other protected demographic characteristic tend to use their cards at pawn shops, massage parlors, and marital counselors more than those who do not share this characteristic, and so whether the policy would have a disparate negative impact based on a protected characteristic. So, what is the right answer? Should the

---

[1] The full list of proxies associated with default also included using the card to pay direct marketing merchants, personal counselors, automobile tire retreading and repair shops, bars and nightclubs, and pool and billiards establishments. (FTC v. CompuCredit 2008).

[2] The FTC's enforcement action, taken under its Section 5 deceptiveness authority, was premised on CompuCredit's misrepresentations about its behavioral scoring model, not on the use of the model itself.

company cut the credit of those who use their card to pay for marital counseling, or not? The solution is anything but clear.

Today, many organizations face ethical choices of this type. Most of these dilemmas do not become public. But some do. For example, Target analyzed customer data to infer which potential customers were pregnant and marketed baby-related goods to them (Duhigg 2012). This provided people with relevant marketing, but it also invaded their privacy. Facebook uses machine learning to predict which of its users are most likely to commit suicide and notifies the police or other first responders when the data suggest that such risk is imminent (Andrade et al. 2018; Marks 2019). Facebook's suicide prevention initiative arguably saves lives. But it can also lead to police knocking on the doors of people who are actually not at risk. Hewlett-Packard used advanced analytics to predict, for each of its 300,000 employees, the likelihood that the person would leave the company, and then provided this "flight risk" score to a select group of managers (Seigel 2016). This could help the company retain valued employees. But it can also prejudice managers against some employees who have no intention of leaving. Should these companies have used in these ways the powerful insights that advanced analytics and AI[3] can provide?

Many of the ethical choices that businesses make with respect to their use of advanced analytics[4] and AI[5] remain hidden from the public eye. But they are there in abundance. Advanced analytics and AI, in combination with the massive amounts of data that the digital society makes available about people, enable data scientists to predict an individual's race, age, IQ, sexual orientation, personality type, substance use, and political views with great accuracy (Kozinski et al. 2013), not to mention their pregnancy status, the likelihood that they will default on their credit card, and many other salient traits. Generative AI (e.g., ChatGPT) raises its own ethical questions such as whether to mine existing, publicly available works to generate new content without compensating the original creators. Advanced analytics and AI give organizations profound new powers that they can use in many ways for their own benefit. Should they feel free to use these technologies in any way that benefits the businesses' short-term interests, or should they observe some limits?

If an organization is to observe some constraints, how should it go about deciding what those limits are? Should it feel free to do anything that the law currently allows?

---

[3] This book will use the term "advanced analytics and AI." However, the term "big data analytics" was more commonly in use at the time that the researchers conducted the interviews and survey and so the interview protocols and survey instruments employed this term. This book will use the "big data analytics" where necessary to represent accurately the survey and interview results.

[4] For the purposes of this book, the term "advanced analytics" refers to "the autonomous or semi-autonomous examination of data or content using sophisticated techniques and tools, typically beyond those of traditional business intelligence (BI), to discover deeper insights, make predictions, or generate recommendations. Advanced analytic techniques include those such as data/text mining, machine learning, pattern matching, forecasting, visualization, semantic analysis, sentiment analysis, network and cluster analysis, multivariate statistics, graph analysis, simulation, complex event processing, neural networks." (Gartner 2023).

[5] As used in this book, the term "artificial intelligence" means the use of "advanced analysis and logic-based techniques, including machine learning, to interpret events, support and automate decisions, and take actions." (Gartner 2023).

Or, should it try to use data and AI ethically and responsibly, even if that means going beyond current legal requirements? If it does seek to achieve an ethical standard, how should it draw the line between ethical and unethical practices? Who in the organization should be responsible for spotting and deciding these issues, where should that person sit in the organization, and what qualifications should they have? What processes should the organization follow for making data ethics decisions? Which internal stakeholders should it consult? Should it engage any external stakeholders?

These questions are at the heart of data ethics management. They are also the subject of this book. Between 2017 and 2019 our interdisciplinary research team interviewed or surveyed 50 or so companies at the forefront of the then-emerging field of "data ethics" management.[6] We found these companies to be struggling with the many ethical dilemmas that the exponential growth in personal data raised for them, and that chief among these were questions about how and whether to use advanced analytics and AI to further their business interests. We learned about how some business organizations wrestle with, and make decisions about, how they will use the newfound power that massive amounts of data about people, used to fuel advanced analytics and AI, have given them. This book conveys what we learned.

We do not write on a blank slate. Much has already been published about the ethical dilemmas that organizations face when they use advanced analytics and AI, and how to govern them. The existing literature takes two main paths. A first group of authors focuses on what it means to use advanced analytics and AI "ethically." Scholars, think tanks, corporations, multi-stakeholder organizations, governments, and others have generated dozens of sets of ethical principles and have encouraged businesses to align their advanced analytics and AI practices with them (Drosou et al. 2017; Gordon and Nyholm 2021; Herschel and Miori 2017; Mcdermott 2017; Mittelstadt et al. 2016; Richards and King 2014; Vallor 2018; Yang et al. 2018; Zwitter 2014). In their review of the global landscape, Jobin and colleagues identified eighty-four such frameworks (Jobin et al. (2019). Fjeld and colleagues surveyed over thirty sets of AI ethics principles put forth by a diverse set of institutions (Fjeld et al. 2020). Though each framework is distinct, it is possible to identify a convergence on a core set of ideas. For example, Jobin and colleagues identified eleven overarching themes: transparency, justice and fairness, non-maleficence, responsibility, privacy, beneficence, freedom and autonomy, trust, dignity, sustainability, and solidarity (Jobin et al. 2019). Floridi and Cowls condensed the multitude of considerations down to five elements: beneficence (promoting well-being and preserving dignity), non-maleficence (ensuring privacy and security), autonomy (avoiding manipulation), justice (preventing unfairness), and explicability (enabling transparency and accountability) (Floridi and Cowls 2019).

While organizations can adopt one of these sets of ethical principles, they tend to have a hard time employing such principles to reach a determinate decision. Consider the question of whether to cut the credit limits of those who seek marital counseling. The "beneficence" principle might counsel in favor of this action since, by pursuing

---

[6] At the time, most organizations called this area "data ethics" management. Today most refer to it as AI ethics or responsible AI management.

it, the company would extend credit to more people who cannot otherwise get it and prevent card holders from taking on too much debt. But it also might push in the other direction since the policy could lead some people to forego marital counseling and its many benefits. And what of the "justice" principle? Is it just to deny credit to someone because they did something that most would view as meritorious such as going to a marriage counselor? High-level ethical principles are good for framing these questions. But they are too often in conflict with one another or too open to interpretation to direct what the answer should be. Taken alone, the existing sets of high-level ethical principles do not provide the necessary guidance.

A second stream of writing seeks to locate the required guidelines in the law. These scholars look to foundational legal frameworks and argue that they should be updated for and applied to business use of advanced analytics and AI. For example, scholars have advocated adopting a "technological due process" approach that takes notions of procedural fairness from the judicial arena and applies them to algorithmic decision-making (Citron 2016; Citron and Pasquale 2014; Crawford and Schultz 2014). Others, drawing on fiduciary law, view corporations that handle people's data as "information fiduciaries" who should put their consumers' or users' interests first, and so become worthy of trust (Balkin 2016; Richards and Hartzog 2015; Waldman 2018b). Another group looks to commercial unfairness law to set parameters for the fair use of predictive analytics (Citron and Pasquale 2014; Hartzog 2015; Hirsch 2015, 2020; MacCarthy 2011). Still others would update legal frameworks to prevent manipulation and harmful bias (Selbst and Barocas 2018; Hellman 2020), promote accountability and transparency, or mandate impact assessments (Selbst 2021).

While these two bodies of scholarship—one focused on ethical principles, the other on legal innovation and reform—are critically important, each would benefit from the addition of a third line of inquiry that, at the time of this study and to a large extent still today, is largely missing from the academic literature: empirical research into what, if anything, companies are doing to manage the threats that their use of advanced analytics and AI can create, and into the strengths and limitations of these management efforts. Scholars have studied these questions with respect to privacy management (Smith 1994; Bamberger and Mulligan 2015; Waldman 2021). While there have been informative accounts of AI governance in practice (Moss and Metcalf 2020), work on this topic is only just beginning.

Empirical knowledge about the practice of AI governance "on the ground" is essential to policymakers who, when designing regulation, must understand how companies implement data governance protections (Bamberger and Mulligan 2015; Waldman 2018a). It also complements the high-level ethical principles by pairing them with an operational understanding of data ethics management and how to motivate it (Whittlestone et al. 2019). Yet too little has been written about whether, how, and why companies go about spotting and preventing the harm that their use of advanced analytics and AI can create.

This book helps to fill this gap. From 2017 to 2019, the research team interviewed and surveyed data governance professionals at US-based companies at the forefront of AI ethics management. The research sought to answer three, fundamental questions: (1) How do business organizations at the forefront of data ethics management conceptualize the threats that their use of advanced analytics and AI create for others, and the ethical challenges that this poses for the organization itself? (2) If it is true that the law does not yet require businesses to reduce these threats, then why, in their own words, are certain companies pursuing this end? (3) How are businesses pursuing data ethics management? Which substantive benchmarks, management structures, processes, and technical solutions do they employ to ground and operationalize their ethical responsibilities as they conceive them?

Gaining insight into these questions provides a novel extension of academic literature that is lacking in empirical investigations (Flyverbom et al. 2019) and contributes to broader conversations among scholars, policymakers and practitioners about how to balance the possibilities and the pitfalls of advanced analytics and AI. While this inquiry overlaps, to some extent, with the other streams of scholarship on ethical principles and regulatory futures, it provides a distinct point of entry focused on how U.S. companies, in their governance of emerging advanced analytics techniques, are interpreting and negotiating a complex, evolving landscape of legislation, regulation, social norms and expectations. The book attempts to explain how a range of professionals tasked with navigating that convergence have articulated both what constitutes responsible decision-making in the uncertain, "beyond compliance" domain of data ethics, and the steps they have taken to achieve this standard.

The researchers used a "grounded theory" approach to understand, and ultimately structure, their findings. Grounded theory is "an organic process of theory emergence based on how well data fit conceptual categories identified by an observer, by how well the categories explain or predict ongoing interpretations, and by how relevant the categories are to the core issues being observed" (Suddaby 2006). In a grounded theory approach, substantive theory provides an initial direction and sensitizes the researchers to certain types of data. But the researchers do not attempt, in a deductive fashion, simply to test the theory against the data. Rather they use a process of "analytic induction" that moves back and forth between deduction and induction "to find the best fit or the most plausible explanation for the relationships being studied" (Suddaby 2006).

This iterative approach led us to conclude that research on the "social license to operate" (Gunningham et al. 2006; Prakash 2011; Bamberger and Mulligan 2015) best fits the behavior that we observed. This body of research has identified a variety of reasons that companies go "beyond compliance" with existing law to signal their conformity with public expectations (Gunningham et al. 2006; Prakash 2011; Bamberger and Mulligan 2015). These reasons include pressures from regulators, consumers, employees, and advocacy organizations, as well as media coverage of controversies. To date, scholarly work on beyond compliance corporate behavior has focused largely on the field of environmental management (Gunningham et al. 2006; Prakash 2011; Short and Toffel 2010). Scholars have also examined corporate responsibility initiatives that seek to improve working conditions and human rights in global supply chains (Bartley 2018; Locke 2013). This book suggests that, in the algorithmic economy, the "social license to operate" increasingly turns on data ethics performance as well. As advanced analytics and AI expand, scholars should look closely at how companies are managing pressures and expectations for fairness, justice, and privacy. Our research suggests that the practice of "data ethics" within companies deals neither exclusively with long-standing questions about data privacy nor with the full range of companies' data uses, but rather with an evolving set of questions about prediction, manipulation, automation, and algorithmic bias. At the same time, not all of these concerns are attended to equally, and companies have pursued a variety of different approaches as they formalize data ethics management.

At least four audiences should find this book to be relevant. The book's description of actual data ethics management practices should be of use to organizations seeking to improve their own performance in this vital management area. Its description of data ethics management "on the ground" (Bamberger and Mulligan 2015) should inform legislators and policymakers attempting to develop workable and effective laws and regulations that build on existing management practices. The book's depiction of beyond compliance data ethics management should further be of interest to scholars that think about the social license to operate and other theories for why organizations may, at times, go beyond legal requirements in the service of social objectives. Finally, by revealing businesses' attempts to govern their own use of advanced analytics and AI, the book hopes to show members of the public that such efforts are possible, even if they may currently be inadequate, and that they should demand and expect more of them.

The book is organized as follows: Chap. 2, *Studying Data Ethics Management: Research Methodology*, describes in greater detail the research team's methods for interviewing and surveying data ethics managers, and for analyzing the data collected. Chapter 3, *Risks: From Privacy and Manipulation to Bias and Displacement*, recounts corporate data governance professionals' assessment of the threats that business use of advanced analytics and AI poses for individuals, groups and the broader society; Chap. 4, *What is Business Data Ethics Management?*, explores what corporate managers mean when they say that they are pursuing "data ethics" as opposed to compliance with privacy or other laws. Chapter 5, *Motivations—Why Do Companies Pursue Data Ethics?* documents the reasons that companies give for pursuing data ethics management, even when the law does not yet require them to do so. Chapter 6, *Drawing Substantive Lines*, discusses the ways in which companies distinguish between ethical, and unethical, uses of advanced analytics and AI, and the benchmarks and standards that they use for this purpose. Chapter 7, *Management Structures and Functions*, identifies who, within a company, is responsible for carrying out the data ethics function, and how this role is structured. Chapter 8, *Management Processes*, discusses the processes that organizations use to spot and ultimately reach decisions about data ethics issues. Chapter 9, *Technical Solutions*, conveys what we learned about the technological and data-focused approaches that companies employ to reduce advanced analytics and AI's potential harms. Chapter 10, *Data Analytics for the Social Good*, describes instances in which companies intentionally use their advanced analytics and AI abilities to serve the social good without any direct benefit to their own bottom lines and explores why they might do this. Chapter 11, *Conclusion*, sums up what we have learned and suggests future directions for research.

# References

Andrade, Gomes De, Norberto Nuno, Dave Pawson, Dan Muriello, Lizzy Donahue, and Jennifer Guadagno. 2018. Ethics and artificial intelligence: suicide prevention on Facebook. *Philosophy & Technology* 31 (4): 669–684.

Balkin, Jack. 2016. Information fiduciaries and the first amendment. *UC Davis Law Review* 49 (4): 1183–1234.

Bamberger, Kenneth A., and Deirdre K. Mulligan. 2015. *Privacy on the Ground: Driving Corporate Behavior in the United States and Europe.* Cambridge, MA: MIT Press.

Bartley, Tim. 2018. *Rules Without Rights: Land, Labor, and Private Authority in the Global Economy.* Oxford: Oxford University Press.

Citron, Danielle Keats. 2016. Big Data Should Be Regulated by 'Technological Due Process.' *The New York Times.* Retrieved April 23, 2020.

Citron, Danielle Keats, and Frank Pasquale. 2014. The scored society: Due process for automated predictions. *Washington Law Review* 89 (1): 1–34.

Crawford, Kate, and Jason Schultz. 2014. Big data and due process: Toward a framework to redress predictive privacy harms. *Boston College Law Review* 55 (1): 93–128.

Drosou, Marina, H.V. Jagadish, Evaggelia Pitoura, and Julia Stoyanovich. 2017. Diversity in big data: A review. *Big Data* 5 (2): 73–84.

Duhigg, Charles. 2012. "*How Companies Learn Your Secrets.*" New York Times (February 16, 2012).

Federal Trade Commission v. CompuCredit Corp. 2008. Complaint. Civil No. 1:08–CV–1976–BBM–RGV. (North. Dist. of Ga., Oct. 8, 2008).

Fjeld, Jessica, Nele Achten, Hannah Hilligoss, Adam Nagy, and Madhulika Srikumar. 2020. *Principled Artificial Intelligence: Mapping Consensus in Ethical and Rights-Based Approaches to Principles for AI.*

Floridi, Luciano, and Josh Cowls. 2019. A unified framework of five principles for AI in society. *Harvard Data Science Review* 1 (1): 1–15.

Flyverbom, Mikkel, Ronald Deibert, and Dirk Matten. 2019. The governance of digital technology, big data, and the Internet: New roles and responsibilities for business. *Business and Society* 58 (1): 3–19.

Gartner, 2023. Glossary. Definition of "advanced analytics" and "artificial intelligence." https://www.gartner.com/en/information-technology/glossary. Accessed August 8, 2023.

Gordon, J.-S., and Sven Nyholm. 2021. Ethics of Artificial Intelligence. Internet Encyclopedia of Philosophy. https://iep.utm.edu/ethic-ai/. Accessed January 15, 2023.

Gunningham, Neil, Robert Kagan and Dorothy Thornton, 2006. Social license and environmental protection: Why businesses go beyond compliance. *Law and Social Inquiry.*

Hartzog, Woodrow. 2015. Unfair and deceptive robots. *Maryland Law Review* 74: 785–829.

Hellman, Deborah. 2020. Measuring algorithmic fairness. *Virginia Law Review* 106: Forthcoming.

Herschel, Richard, and Virginia M. Miori. 2017. Ethics & big data. *Technology in Society* 49: 31–36.

Hirsch, Dennis D. 2015. That's unfair! Or is it? Big data, discrimination and the FTC's unfairness authority. *Kentucky Law Journal* 103: 345–361.

Hirsch, Dennis D. 2020. From individual control to social protection: New paradigms for law and policy in the age of predictive analytics. *Maryland Law Review* 79: 439–505.

Jobin, Anna, Marcello Ienca, and Effy Vayena. 2019. The global landscape of AI ethics guidelines. *Nature Machine Intelligence* 1: 389–399.

Kozinski, Michael, David Stillwell, and Thore Graepel. 2013. Private traits and attributes are predictable from digital records of human behavior. *Proceedings of the National Academy of Sciences* 110 (15): 5802–5805.

Locke, Richard M. 2013. *The Promise and Limits of Private Power: Promoting Labor Standards in a Global Economy.* Cambridge: Cambridge University Press.

MacCarthy, Mark. 2011. New directions in privacy: Disclosure, unfairness and externalities. *I/S: Journal of Law and Policy for the Information Society* 6 (3): 425–512.

# References

Marks, Mason. 2019. Artificial intelligence based suicide prediction. *Yale Journal of Law and Technology* 21 (3): 98–121.

Mcdermott, Yvonne. 2017. Conceptualising the right to data protection in an era of big data. *Big Data & Society* (January–June): 1–7.

Mittelstadt, Brent D., Patrick Allo, Mariarosaria Taddeo, Sandra Wachter, and Luciano Floridi. 2016. The ethics of algorithms: Mapping the debate. *Big Data and Society* 3 (2): 1–21.

Moss, Emanuel, and Jacob Metcalf. 2020. *Ethics Owners: A New Model of Organizational Responsibility in Data-Driven Technology Companies*, 2020. New York: Data & Society Research Institute.

Prakash, Aseem. 2011. Why do firms adopt 'beyond compliance' environmental policies. *Business Strategy and the Environment* 10: 286–299.

Richards, Neil M., and Jonathan H. King. 2014. Big data ethics. *Wake Forest Law Review* 49 (2): 393–432.

Richards, Neil M., and Woodrow Hartzog. 2015. Taking trust seriously in privacy law. *Stanford Technology Law Review* 19: 431–472.

Selbst, Andrew D. 2021. An institutional view of algorithmic impact assessments. *Harvard Journal of Law & Technology* 35 (1): 117–191.

Selbst, Andrew D., and Solon Barocas. 2018. The intuitive appeal of explainable machines. *Fordham Law Review* 87 (3): 1085–1139.

Short, Jodi L., and Michael W. Toffel. 2010. Making self-regulation more than merely symbolic: The critical role of the legal environment. *Administrative Science Quarterly* 55 (3): 361–396.

Siegel, Eric. 2016. *Predictive Analytics: The Power to Predict Who Will Click, Buy, Lie or Die*. Hoboken, New Jersey: John Wiley & Sons.

Smith, H. Jeff. 1994. *Managing Privacy: Information Technology and Corporate America*. Chapel Hill, NC: University of North Carolina Press.

Suddaby, Roy. 2006. From the editors: What grounded theory is not. *Academy of Management Journal* 49 (4): 633–642.

Vallor, Shannon. 2018. *An Introduction to Data Ethics (Course Module)*. Santa Clara, CA: Markkula Center for Applied Ethics.

Waldman, Ari E. 2018a. Designing without privacy. *Houston Law Review* 55 (3): 659–727.

Waldman, Ari E. 2018b. *Privacy as Trust: Information Privacy for an Information Age*. Cambridge University Press.

Waldman, Ari E. 2021. *Industry Unbound: The Inside Story of Privacy, Data and Corporate Power*. Cambridge, UK: Cambridge University Press.

Whittlestone, Jess, Rune Nyrup, Anna Alexandrova, and Stephen Cave. 2019. The role and limits of principles in AI ethics: Towards a focus on tensions. In *Proceedings of the 2019 AAAI/ACM Conference on AI, Ethics, and Society*, 195–200.

Yang, Ke, Julia Stoyanovich, Abolfazl Asudeh, Bill Howe, H. V. Jagadish, and Gerome Miklau. 2018. A nutritional label for rankings. In *Proceedings of the International Conference on Management of Data (SIGMOD'18)*, 1773–1776.

Zwitter, Andrej. 2014. Big data ethics. *Big Data & Society* (July–December): 1–6.

**Open Access** This chapter is licensed under the terms of the Creative Commons Attribution 4.0 International License (http://creativecommons.org/licenses/by/4.0/), which permits use, sharing, adaptation, distribution and reproduction in any medium or format, as long as you give appropriate credit to the original author(s) and the source, provide a link to the Creative Commons license and indicate if changes were made.

The images or other third party material in this chapter are included in the chapter's Creative Commons license, unless indicated otherwise in a credit line to the material. If material is not included in the chapter's Creative Commons license and your intended use is not permitted by statutory regulation or exceeds the permitted use, you will need to obtain permission directly from the copyright holder.

# Chapter 2
# Studying Data Ethics Management: Research Methodology

**Abstract** This chapter outlines our approach to investigating how corporations manage the threats and risks that their use of advanced analytics can create. Specifically, we deploy a mixed method research design combining insights from semi-structured interviews and an original survey of business data ethics managers as well as the attorneys, consultants, and think tanks who advise them. The interviews and survey hone in on five key areas of inquiry: (1) the risks big data can create, (2) motivations for why businesses attempt to mitigate the risks of big data when the law does not yet require them do so, (3) how businesses manage these risks via frameworks, management processes, and/or technological solutions, (4) how businesses attempt to use advanced analytics and AI for the social good, and (5) the broader regulatory and legal environment within which data ethics management operates. By using multiple research methods and focusing on multiple dimensions of corporate use of analytics, our analysis provides an entrée into the state of the art of data ethics management.

**Keywords** AI research · Mixed methods · Snowball sampling

> **Key Take-Aways**
>
> - **Mixed methods research**. This study employs a mixed-methods research design that includes interviews with, and a survey of, business data ethics managers and the think tanks, attorneys, and consultants who advise them.
> - **Five main areas of inquiry**. The interview protocol and survey instrument focused on five main areas of inquiry: (1) the risks that business use of big data can create; (2) why businesses seek to mitigate the risks of big data when the law does not yet require them to do so; (3) how businesses go about managing these risks, including their use of substantive frameworks, management structures and processes, and technological solutions; (4) business attempts to use advanced analytics and AI for the social good;

© The Author(s) 2024
D. Hirsch et al., *Business Data Ethics*,
SpringerBriefs in Law,
https://doi.org/10.1007/978-3-031-21491-2_2

and (5) the broader regulatory and legal environment within which data ethics management operates.
- **Snowball sampling**. The researchers used a snowball sampling method to identify and interview twenty-three subjects. They distributed the survey through five industry-oriented trade associations and think tanks and received 51 responses, with 24 of them being fully complete.
- **Skewed sample**. The survey sample skewed towards larger organizations, and focused on companies in the information technology, financial services, communications, industrial, and healthcare sectors.
- **State of the art, not best practice**. The research focused on why businesses were pursuing data ethics management, and what they were doing in this regard. It did not evaluate these activities and so does not identify *best* practices.

We employ a mixed-methods research design, including in-depth interviews with, and a survey of, business data ethics managers and the think tanks, attorneys, and consultants who advise them. The interview component served as an open-ended way to map the terrain of the contestation around big data ethics and inform the construction of a meaningful survey instrument. The survey component sought to synthesize insights from the interviews and so to understand how systematically to assess business uses of big data, the risks, and the specific policies and processes intended to address those risks. We treat the research components as complementary, collectively contributing unique dimensions to our empirical investigation of business practices for addressing the risks of advanced analytics and AI. Targeting higher-level executives for our interviews and survey gives us the view of business practices from the top, but precludes us from assessing the coupling between high-level policies and the actual daily work of engineers and employees on the ground (Waldman 2018). Likewise, our survey sampling methodology, discussed more below, lends itself to selection bias. The Ohio State University Institutional Review Board deemed the research exempt from further review.

## 2.1 Interviews

For the interviews, we used a purposive sampling method in which we leveraged the research team's social networks to identify individuals prominently engaged in managing the risks that business use of advanced analytics and AI can create, and the professionals (lawyers, consultants, think tanks, thought leaders) who advise them (Singleton and Straits 2010). We then snowball sampled by asking interviewees to identify additional individuals who were highly knowledgeable about the business practice of big data ethics management or were actively grappling with big data ethics in their positions. The snowball method facilitated access to new interviewees. This proved to be important as reaching high-level managers is particularly challenging (Biernacki and Waldorf 1981; Cycyota and Harrison 2002).

The interview protocol was developed to probe respondents broadly about big data ethics in the business context. The protocol had four major sections: (1) risks of big data, (2) motivations and goals of mitigating the risks of big data, (3) management processes, substantive frameworks, and technological solutions for mitigating these risks, (4) whether businesses seek to use advanced analytics and AI for the social good in ways that do not directly impact the bottom line; and (5) the broader regulatory and legal environment within which data ethics management takes place. The protocol was adjusted to account for differences between types of organizations for which the interviewees worked: businesses that use advanced analytics and AI, law firms, think tanks, and consulting firms. When interviewing representatives of business organizations that used advanced analytics and AI, our interviews probed respondents on the structure, design, and perceived efficacy of internal processes. Interviews were conducted primarily over the phone (with one interview conducted in person) from September 2017 to March 2019. Interviews ranged from 60 to 160 min with an average of 75 min. We transcribed interviews to facilitate coding and analysis which involved descriptive coding according to the sections of interviews followed by close readings to identify prevalent themes across interviews.

Overall, we interviewed 23 respondents. The industries represented in the interview sample include telecommunications, information technology, social media, pharmaceuticals, and insurance. Both publicly traded and private companies are represented in the sample. The interviewee's titles included, at various levels of seniority: Privacy Officer, Data Ethics Officer, Counsel, Public Policy Executive, Compliance Executive, and Partner.

## 2.2 Survey

We paired the interview study with an online survey that we designed and conducted using the Qualtrics platform. As with the interview component, we targeted higher-level management. Accessing this type of population with large-scale probability sampling methods is notoriously difficult (Cycyota and Harrison 2002). Survey research of corporate management has indicated that an important way to increase response rates is to have the survey delivered through legitimated or trusted organizations. As a result, we opted for a convenience sampling approach that leveraged the social networks of corporations through membership in industry trade associations and industry-funded think tanks.

Specifically, five industry-oriented trade organizations and think tanks engaged with issues of data and privacy sent our survey to their member companies.[1] Given

---

[1] These organizations were the Centre for Information Policy Leadership (CIPL), the Computer and Communications Industry Association (CCIA), the Future of Privacy Forum (FPF), the Information Accountability Foundation (IAF), and the Software and Information Industry Association (SIIA).

that this targeted sample selected into membership in organizations engaged with privacy and data accountability, our survey results likely provide a more optimistic view of current corporate practices than a larger or more random sample would have offered.. We provided the think tanks and trade organizations with email language/script and survey links for their members and made sure that companies that belonged to more than one of these organizations received only one survey link. The think tanks and trade organizations agreed to send reminder emails one week after the initial survey was sent. Data was collected from November 2019 to January 2020.

In total, our survey was sent to 246 companies. We received a total of 51 responses with 24 fully completed yielding a response rate of approximately 20% for all surveys and approximately 10% for fully completed surveys. This response rate is fairly consistent with other surveys of corporate managers (Cycyota and Harrison 2006). Given our targeted sampling strategy and exploratory nature of the study, we are unable to make strong claims. However, we can identify cleavages of variation and associations that will serve as an important entry point for future research. In particular, our findings from this targeted survey provide evidence that a much larger sampling of corporate big data ethics is necessary and would likely yield valuable insights for scholars, policymakers and business organizations.

We derive our survey results, presented below, from our "core sample" of 31 respondents who answered our survey question about the policies their company has in place to address the risks of advanced analytics and AI (22 of these respondents fully completed the survey). Figures 2.1 and 2.2 display the variation in company size in our sample by number of employees and revenue, respectively. We expected that our sample would be comprised of larger companies on average given the membership of the organizations through which we developed our sample, and this indeed turned out to be the case. The largest proportion of the sample, approximately 30%, have more than 40,000 employees or more than $15 billion in revenue. While skewed towards large companies, almost 50% of the sample has fewer than 10,000 employees. As it relates to industries, Table 2.1 shows that most of our corporate respondents worked for information technology companies, with the remainder working for financial services, communications, industrial and healthcare companies, with healthcare composing the smallest proportion of the core sample.

In subsequent chapters, we will draw from both our survey and interviews to illustrate the array of different concerns, rationales, policies, and systems that are central to data ethics management in these types of corporations.

## 2.2 Survey

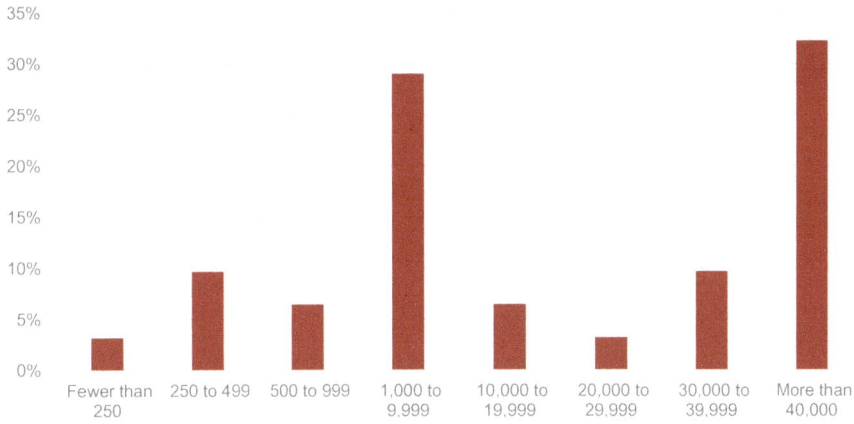

**Fig. 2.1** Distribution of sample company size according to total number of employees

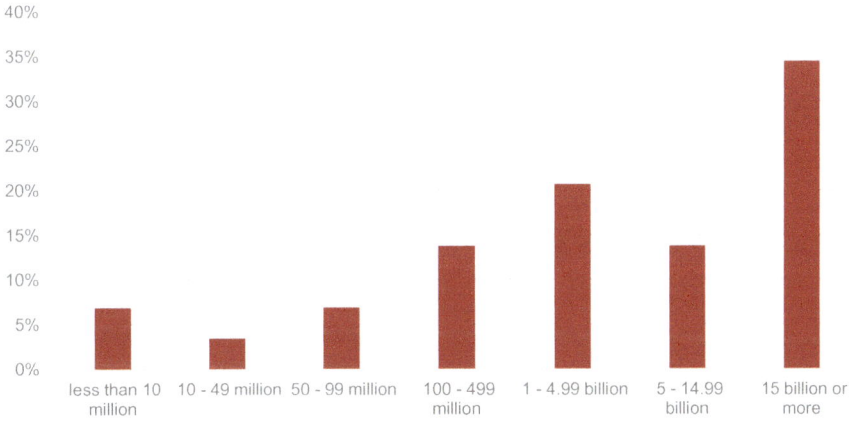

**Fig. 2.2** Distribution of sample company size according to 2018 revenue

**Table 2.1** Survey respondent industry

|  | Percent |
| --- | --- |
| Communications services (including telecommunication services and media and entertainment, including advertising) | 16.1 |
| Information technology (including software and services, technology hardware and equipment, and semiconductors and semiconductor equipment) | 41.9 |
| Financials (including banks, diversified financials, and insurance) | 16.1 |
| Health care (including health care equipment and services and pharmaceuticals, biotechnology and life sciences) | 9.7 |
| Industrials (including commercial and professional services, human resource and employment services, office services, capital goods, and transportation) | 16.1 |

# References

Biernacki, Patrick, and Dan Waldorf. 1981. Snowball sampling: Problems and techniques of chain referral sampling. *Sociological Methods & Research* 10 (2): 141–163.

Cycyota, Cynthia S., and David A. Harrison. 2002. Enhancing survey response rates at the executive level: Are employee- or consumer-level techniques effective ? *Journal of Management* 28 (2): 151–176.

Cycyota, Cynthia S., and David A. Harrison. 2006. What (not to expect a meta-analysis of top manager response rates and techniques over time. *Organizational Research Methods* 9 (2): 133–160.

Singleton, Royce A., and Bruce C. Straits. 2010. *Approaches to Social Research*. New York: Oxford University Press.

Waldman, Ari E. 2018. Designing without privacy. *Houston Law Review* 55 (3): 659–727.

**Open Access** This chapter is licensed under the terms of the Creative Commons Attribution 4.0 International License (http://creativecommons.org/licenses/by/4.0/), which permits use, sharing, adaptation, distribution and reproduction in any medium or format, as long as you give appropriate credit to the original author(s) and the source, provide a link to the Creative Commons license and indicate if changes were made.

The images or other third party material in this chapter are included in the chapter's Creative Commons license, unless indicated otherwise in a credit line to the material. If material is not included in the chapter's Creative Commons license and your intended use is not permitted by statutory regulation or exceeds the permitted use, you will need to obtain permission directly from the copyright holder.

# Chapter 3
# Risks: From Privacy and Manipulation to Bias and Displacement

**Abstract** This chapter leverages findings from both our semi-structured interviews and original survey to discuss the types of risks central to how data ethics managers and their advisors think about advanced analytics and AI. Both survey respondents and interview participants highlighted a broad range of concerns raised by their use of advanced analytics ranging from invasion of privacy and manipulation to bias against protected classes and concerns about power imbalances. While the risks were wide ranging, some risks received more attention than others. Respondents were far more focused on privacy, bias, errors and problems of opacity than on concerns of manipulation or the negative effects technology can have on displacing labor. Understanding the variation in the types of concerns and the unevenness in attention to different risks is critical as such variation likely lends itself to differences in the types of processes and structures organizations develop to manage those risks.

**Keywords** Data risks · AI risks · Algorithmic discrimination · Privacy · Unfairness · Manipulation

**Key Take-Aways**

- Private sector data ethics managers, and those that advise them, reported that business use of advanced analytics and AI can pose important risks to individuals and the broader society. When viewed in concert with the benefits to the business and to society that these same practices can create, this can pose ethical dilemmas and challenges. The interviewees identified the following risks associated with business use of advanced analytics and AI:
  - **Invasion of privacy**: Companies can use advanced analytics to take seemingly innocuous surface data about people and infer from it highly sensitive, latent information.

- **Manipulation**: Companies can use the information that they infer about people to manipulate them. Particularly bad actors can infer people's vulnerabilities and then leverage this information to exploit these individuals.
- **Bias against protected classes**: Algorithmic systems can discriminate on the basis of a protected classification (race, gender, religion, etc.). This can occur where the data set includes such classifications, or where facially neutral training data, shaped by past bias, produces models that have negative, disparate impacts on groups defined by a protected characteristic.
- **Increased power imbalances**: Advanced analytics can give businesses far more insight into their customers than their customers have into them, and so can produce a power imbalance between businesses and their customers.
- **Error**: Inaccurate data or faulty algorithms can produce erroneous models and predictions that can negatively impact people.
- **Opacity and procedural unfairness**: Most people lack an understanding of, and opportunities to challenge, the corporate algorithmic determinations that can shape their life opportunities.
- **Displacement of labor**: Advanced analytics facilitates increased automation which, in turn, can displace human labor.
- **Pressure to conform**: Individuals may feel pressure to conform to behaviors that they think will please the algorithmic decision-maker.
- **Intentional, harmful use**: AI and the powerful products that it enables, such as facial recognition tools, can intentionally be put to harmful use.

- Data ethics managers were far more focused on privacy, bias, error, and opacity risks than on issues such as manipulation or labor displacement.

The research team's exploration of data ethics management included an inquiry into the risks—to individuals, groups, and society as a whole—that such management efforts sought to address. Nearly everyone we surveyed and interviewed acknowledged that business use of advanced analytics poses such risks, and that it is important for companies to address them. The survey and interview components of the research project each utilized small samples shaped by selection bias, so they can tell us only about a specific set of companies. Still, their consistency on the question of risks is striking.[1] At the time that we collected our data, most companies that talked publicly about their use of advanced analytics focused on the valuable insights that it produces. The survey and interviews suggested that this rosy view was only part of the picture and that some of the more sophisticated companies, at least, also recognized the very real threats that these activities create.

---

[1] Others have published lists of risks from AI (Future of Privacy Forum 2017). For the most part, they align with those that our respondents identified.

## 3.1 Privacy Violations

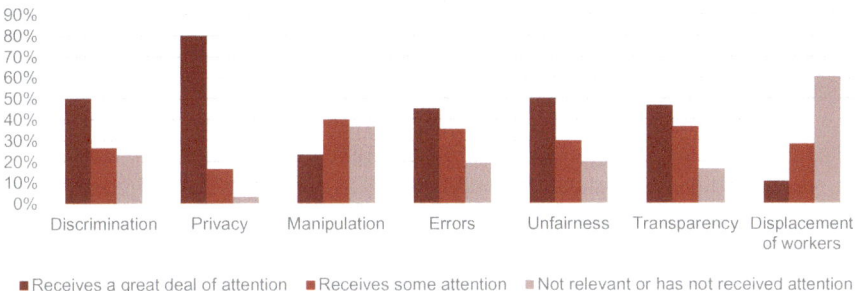

**Fig. 3.1** Corporate attention to risks from advanced analytics

While survey respondents acknowledged a broad range of risks, they reported that their companies pay far more attention to some risks than others, as illustrated in Fig. 3.1.

Eighty percent of respondents said that companies pay a great deal of attention to the privacy risks that advanced analytics creates. Nearly half said that businesses pay a great deal of attention to risks of discrimination or bias, unfairness (e.g., predictions that might bring undue harm to consumers or employees), lack of transparency or accountability (e.g., through opaque algorithms), and, to a slightly lesser extent, to errors in decision making. On the other hand, the respondents reported far less attention to risks of manipulation (e.g., of consumers or users of a service), and an especially low level of attention to risks of worker displacement through automation, which most respondents rated as essentially irrelevant. Interestingly, while more than 60% of respondents saw risks of manipulation as relevant to business use of advanced analytics and AI, they most commonly rated this as having received just some attention rather than a great deal of attention. This is surprising given that the highest-profile breach of data ethics—the Facebook-Cambridge Analytica incident—involved the use of advanced analytics to manipulate voters.

Our interviews allow for a closer look at how businesses perceive these risks, as well as an even broader array of concerns about how business use of advanced analytics and AI could be harmful to individuals and societies.

## 3.1 Privacy Violations

Companies can use advanced analytics to take seemingly innocuous surface data about people and infer highly sensitive information from it with high levels of accuracy. For example, researchers at Cambridge University were able to take a person's Facebook likes and infer their gender, sexuality, age, race, and political affiliation "with remarkable accuracy" based solely on these surface data (Rosen 2013). Predictive analytics thus poses a profound threat to personal privacy (Rubinstein 2013). The interviewees expressed keen awareness of this threat to privacy. As one remarked:

"You're learning my weaknesses or learning my pregnancy status, you're learning whether I'm gay, you're learning intimate information about what I do in my home. Is it ethical for you to be doing that even though your policy said you do research and we collect that information for product improvement?" (Interviewee #19).

The interviewees distinguished between different types or levels of privacy invasion. Some predictive insights feel "creepy," such as when Facebook inferred which of its users were Jewish and sent Rosh Hashanah (Jewish New Year) greetings to them (Interviewee #23). Other insights are more invasive and can cause severe embarrassment, distress or even danger. For example, some gay teens have been outed to their parents as a result of their receiving gay-themed advertising from companies that inferred their sexual orientation (Interviewee #23). Finally, companies may deny people opportunities for jobs, loans or other important life opportunities based on predictive insights about their physical or mental health status, sexual orientation or other highly personal attributes. One interviewee gave the example of a producer of smart toothbrushes that faced economic pressure to sell household tooth brushing data to insurance companies who could infer risk of heart disease from it. "This might go to future insurability of the kids or payment for pre-existing condition of the adults. My point is, the world is changing and measurement or observation of us, which is happening, this is the way it all works, is very, very important. We've got to decide what the rules are now. Right?" (Interviewee #6).

## 3.2 Manipulation

Data scientists can employ advanced analytics to infer people's vulnerabilities. This can allow bad actors to manipulate, or even exploit, these individuals. For example, a business might predict that an individual is likely to experience early-stage dementia and target the person with predatory loans intended to take advantage of her diminished, but undiagnosed, mental state. Or, as actually happened, a company such as Cambridge Analytica might take people's Facebook "likes," use them to infer their personality types, and then target them with political advertisements that appeal to their unconscious in ways that they find hard to resist (Rosenberg 2018).[2] One interviewee saw such manipulation as a growing issue:

> [P]eople are becoming more sensitive to some of the risks that I might put into the category of being unfairly manipulative, or kind of unfair in some way. That might be using predictive analytics to sell people things they don't need or can't really afford. Or, targeting people based on vulnerabilities, whether it's age, or cognitive abilities, or some other disability . . . . When you see them happening . . . people recoil as slimy and nobody

---

[2] An interviewee explained how this issue can arise on the smart retail environment where sensors, including those placed in the mirrors at beauty counters, can infer from shoppers' facial expressions their likelihood of buying a particular good. The store can then market that good to the individual in real-time in the store. "I'm not saying that we're there, I'm not saying that anybody is necessarily there. But I think that's where we're going." (Interviewee #16).

wants to be that.... When do those lines get crossed? So that's not always obvious. There's certainly a sensitivity around that. (Interviewee #12).

The difficult questions lie in identifying the point at which marketing becomes unacceptable manipulation, or even exploitation. An interviewee from the retail industry talked about how they approach this issue:

How much imputation can you do before you're actually manipulating and defining the behavior and causing the behavior, rather than responding to it? ... I've said this a lot to our marketing teams. I was like, "so long as you are persuading." In your gut, [if you] know that you are persuading and providing an offer, and something of value -- you're good. The moment you feel that you are manipulating, you've gone too far, and we need to have a conversation. (Interviewee #17).

This gut-level, know-it-when-you-see-it approach to drawing the line between marketing and unacceptable manipulation leaves a great deal of room for interpretation.

## 3.3 Bias Against Protected Classes

The law distinguishes between disparate *treatment* and disparate *impact* discrimination. Disparate treatment occurs when one intentionally and deliberately disadvantages another based on a protected characteristic (e.g., race, or gender). Disparate impact occurs when a policy or practice that is neutral on its face disproportionately and negatively affects a group of people defined by a protected characteristic (race, sex, religion, etc.) where there is no legitimate business necessity for the practice, or where there is a legitimate business purpose but there is a less-discriminatory way of achieving it.

Advanced analytics and AI can produce disparate treatment. For example, a company could infer someone's protected characteristic (e.g., pregnancy), and intentionally discriminate against the person on this basis.[3] The more likely scenario is for the use of these technologies to produce disparate impact discrimination. For example, reliance on training data that has itself been shaped by past bias can produce a model that replicates and perpetuates that bias. Amazon ran into this when it tried to develop an AI tool that could separate viable from non-viable resumes (Dastin 2018). It trained the tool on the resumes of existing Amazon employees most of whom–likely due to pre-existing bias in the technology field–were male. The tool accordingly learned to reject applicants whose resumes identified them as female (e.g., by listing an all-women's college). Amazon discovered this problem early on and, unable to fix it, ultimately abandoned the project. But bias in the training data can be subtle and many companies may miss it.

---

[3] Such a practice would likely violate employment discrimination laws, *see* e.g., The Pregnancy Discrimination Act of 1978, amending Title VII of the Civil Rights Act of 1964, 42 U.S.C. § 2000e (prohibiting an employer from discriminating against an employee or applicant based on pregnancy status), but would be very hard to detect.

Harmful bias seemed to be one of the top, if not the top, concern of the interviewees:

> Algorithmic discrimination is a top tier issue for me and my group, and I've made it a priority. What I mean by that is to work, and help, and focus, our engineering teams on evaluating outcomes as we build out especially our machine learning portfolio. You're never going to be able to be 100 percent positive, in a testing environment, that your algorithm isn't creating some disparate impact. That's very difficult to do . . . How do you get data that doesn't have a lot of bias in it? That's also tricky, but there's some data sets that we all know to have tremendous bias in it, so maybe steering away from those insofar as you're training the models might be helpful, right? (Interviewee #18).

Increasingly, companies seek to address the problem of algorithmic bias by seeking to identify, and either not use or modify, biased data sets. This is an important strategy. The ethical question that the interviewees posed was how far to go with this. Specifically, do companies have an obligation to "fix" long-standing social inequalities that are accurately reflected in the training data? For example, should a facial recognition tool that learned it could identify gender in part by whether the person was standing in a kitchen (women were more likely to be in the kitchen) deliberately ignore this finding? (Interviewee #19). If women, through their online behavior, express less interest in certain high-paid jobs than men, should a company nonetheless advertise the jobs equally to both women and men? (Interviewee #19). Should the company ignore or alter the training data in these cases, or modify the conclusions that emerged from it? The interviewees talked with their data scientists about this question. As one explained, "[t]he concern is now you've taught this thing, this code, to be biased. On the other hand, do they have some obligation to have the algorithm be less accurate... do you want me to pull [those data that are the product of bias] out? So these sorts of questions are being asked of us by the AI folks: 'We'll figure out how to do or not do... but tell us when and where prediction is discriminatory in a way that is to be deterred.'" (Interviewee #19).

Another grey area was when, if ever, it is acceptable to use a protected characteristic in algorithmic decision-making. For example, when data shows that different racial or ethnic groups have different preferences, is it appropriate to take this into account in marketing to the members of these groups? An interviewee from the retail industry provided an example:

> So we know that there's different body sizes, or different body types perhaps, for different ethnicities. You might need wider-thighed jeans. We're conscious of that. And again, this is just matching the customer with what they need. So in that case, if we have a special on jeans and we want to make sure they're the right jeans, that ethnic code might actually be important. (Interviewee #17)

These interviews raise deep and interesting questions about what a society that values equality and justice should look like, and about what companies should do to try to achieve that vision. They suggest that at least some corporate privacy professionals and data scientists are discussing these issues but are doing so without the benefit of well-developed tools, resources or ethical frameworks that could help them navigate the grey areas.

## 3.4 Increased Power Imbalances

Businesses that employ advanced analytics to achieve highly accurate insights into their customers can use this to build an advantage over them. For example, a company could infer the highest price that each customer would be willing to pay for a given good or service, and then charge the individual that price. This would allow the company to capture all the gains from trade. Additionally, corporate use of advanced analytics to determine eligibility for loans, jobs or other important opportunities can entrench existing inequalities. If more privileged applicants are more likely to possess the attributes (proxies) that predict job success or loan repayment, the algorithm will more likely select them for these opportunities. This can reproduce existing hierarchies and further lock the poor into poverty. Advanced analytics and AI can further enable companies to segment groups into much finer categories than was previously possible. This can have social and distributional effects. For example, it can undermine the pooling of risk that has long been one of the social functions of insurance. In each of these ways, the increased use of advanced analytics and AI can produce, and reproduce, inequality.

## 3.5 Error

Inaccurate data or faulty algorithms can produce erroneous predictions. In the marketing area, such errors can result in annoyed or dissatisfied customers (Interviewee #12). In the government context, the stakes can be much higher. As one interviewee recounted: "Our number one risk is if someone is killed because of our analytics. We're working with the military, we're working with intelligence and law enforcement, and I've impressed this on the engineers a number of times, you're pointing a loaded gun at someone basically. Are we 100% confident in the analysis that we're supporting here, and if we're not, then the consequences are that level of seriousness." (Interviewee #10).

## 3.6 Opacity and Procedural Unfairness

While it is true that algorithmic decision-makers can make errors, the same can be said for human decision-makers. The key distinction between algorithmic and human decision-making is not the former's capacity for error, but rather its opacity and imperviousness to challenge. For example, where a company determines through advanced analytics that an employee would not succeed in a higher position and denies the person a promotion, the employee would have no way to know what data or algorithm had resulted in this determination, and no way to challenge them (Rubinstein 2013). Such algorithmic determinations are a "black box" as far as the individual is concerned. (Pasquale 2016). In some advanced machine learning, even the company or other decision-maker may not understand how the technology arrived at its determination. The risk to the individual, then, is that machine-driven decisions deny people the core procedural rights—transparency and the right to be heard—to which they are entitled when others are making important decisions about their lives. One interviewee articulated this risk:

> In this case, if a harm occurs, there is no mechanism to even understand why suddenly am I on the No Fly List. . . . How did I get on the No Fly List? There is no mechanism to ask. You will be told, "[it's] none of your business, you simply can't fly anymore." . . . What if [the list placement] was because in the third generation of processing, where they were not using data about me but data inferred about me, something got in there that was a horrible inaccuracy or trigger and now it is perpetuated because suddenly, it's no longer about the data about me, it's about data that has been inferred about me. Some risk score. And there is no mechanism to actually understand why [it happened] or to have [the data] corrected. (Interviewee #21).

## 3.7 Displacement of Labor

Advanced analytics facilitates increased automation which, in turn, can displace the existing, human labor force. As one interviewee explained:

> The thing that worries me enormously in this way is driverless cars. . . . You're going to put people out of work: trucking, cab drivers, low skill workers, people who aren't going to be able to get other jobs and I don't think the industry thinks it has to care about that. The speed at which it's developing these things, if it builds a driverless car that works really well and starts replacing everybody before society is able to figure out what are we going to do with all these people that it's displaced . . . that's hugely irresponsible. That's the kind of thing that topples governments, leads to the French Revolution, you know? This is significant, and I don't think industry really takes responsibility for that . . . And what's the legal solution? Ban driverless cars? Maybe, but that's a hard call. What's the rationale for that? I think these are the huge challenges that engineers have to own; but I'm not sure they know they should. (Interviewee #10).

## 3.8 Pressure to Conform

One interviewee expressed a deep fear that constant data collection about people, combined with analysis of that data to allocate goods and opportunities, would create a profound pressure on individuals to conform to behaviors that they think will please the algorithmic decision-maker.

> [M]y biggest fear, which is almost Orwellian, is that . . . [a]t some point, we as individuals will begin to realize that we are being observed. And everything about our behaviors and our patterns of behaviors are being understood, compiled, inferences are being created. And there will be a point in time in the near future . . . where we're going to internalize that. And you know what's going to happen . . . we are going to be the person we think people want us to be all the time. And what impact is that going to have on creativity? What impact is that

going to have in ultimately funneling us all down into behavior that we believe or, worse case, know that we must conform to? . . . What impact is that going to have on society? On culture? On us as individuals? It scares the hell out of me. And it's happening right now. (Interviewee #21).

## 3.9 Intentional, Harmful Use of Analytics

Some companies worried that customers or others would use their analytic tools for morally problematic ends. For example, one company had an internal debate about whether to sell its technology to customers that may have ties to the Chinese government which might use the technology to create facial recognition tools capable of distinguishing members of the Uighur minority (Interviewee #2).[4] In a well-publicized 2018 incident, thousands of Google employees signed a letter protesting the company's work on a Pentagon pilot program, Project Maven, which used machine learning to interpret drone imagery and, potentially, to better target drone strikes against suspected terrorists or other individuals (Wakabayashi and Shane 2018). The letter expressed the employees' view that "Google should not be in the business of war." A few months later, Google announced that it would cease its involvement with the controversial Pentagon program (Harwell 2018).

The difficult question is where to draw the line. One interviewee described an employee complaint about the company's analytic work for a cosmetics manufacturer. "[S]omebody sent an email to me and they said, 'What good does it do the world to perpetuate working with companies whose primary mission is to make women feel bad about how they look?' I thought about the question, it's not really a civil liberties or privacy question, but we didn't feel like we should ignore it, so we started having a conversation... but this was interesting: how do we evaluate?" (Interviewee #10). The lines are not clear. Even the question of whether to do advanced analytics work for the Pentagon has no obvious answer. Several months after Google's announcement on Project Maven, Microsoft and Amazon separately affirmed their willingness to contribute to the Department of Defense's AI efforts. (Gregg 2018).

While it is commonplace today to think about the harm that advanced analytics and AI can create, that was not as common a view at the time of the interviews and survey on which this book is based. As the above discussion makes clear, the companies that we studied were aware of these risks. That, in turn, raised the question of what a company should do to address them. Was compliance with existing legal requirements sufficient? Or should a company go beyond this? It is to that question that we now turn.

---

[4] This interview, and the internal debate to which the interviewee referred, took place prior to the United States' decision to add these Chinese companies to the Entity List, and so to prohibit U.S. companies from exporting certain items to them without a license on the grounds that doing so could compromise U.S. national security. *See* U.S. Dept. of Commerce, Bureau of Industry and Security, Addition of Certain Entities to the Entity List, 84 Fed. Reg. 54,002 (Oct. 9, 2019). Thus, at the time of the internal debate referred to, it was still legal for U.S. companies to export to these Chinese companies.

## References

Dastin, Jeffrey. 2018. Amazon scraps secret AI recruiting tool that showed bias against women. *Reuters* (October 9, 2018).

Gregg, Aaron. 2018. Microsoft, Amazon pledge to work with pentagon following anonymous online rebukes. *The Washington Post* (October 26, 2018).

Harwell, Drew. 2018. Google to drop pentagon AI contract after employee objections to the 'business of war'. *The Washington Post* (June 1, 2018).

Pasquale, Frank. 2016. *The Black Box Society: The Secret Algorithms That Control Money and Information*. Cambridge: Harvard University Press.

Rosen, Rebecca J. 2013. Armed with facebook 'likes' alone, researchers can tell your race, gender, and sexual orientation. *The Atlantic* (March 12, 2013).

Rosenberg, Matthew, et al. 2018. How trump consultants exploited the Facebook data of millions. *New York Times* (March 17, 2018).

Rubinstein, Ira S. 2013. Big data: The end of privacy or a new beginning? *International Data Privacy Law* 3 (2): 74–87.

Shane, Scott, and Daisuke Wakabayashi. 2018. 'The business of war,' Google employees protest work for the pentagon. *New York Times* (April 4, 2018).

**Open Access** This chapter is licensed under the terms of the Creative Commons Attribution 4.0 International License (http://creativecommons.org/licenses/by/4.0/), which permits use, sharing, adaptation, distribution and reproduction in any medium or format, as long as you give appropriate credit to the original author(s) and the source, provide a link to the Creative Commons license and indicate if changes were made.

The images or other third party material in this chapter are included in the chapter's Creative Commons license, unless indicated otherwise in a credit line to the material. If material is not included in the chapter's Creative Commons license and your intended use is not permitted by statutory regulation or exceeds the permitted use, you will need to obtain permission directly from the copyright holder.

# Chapter 4
# What is Business Data Ethics Management?

**Abstract** The law, including privacy law, lags the rapid development of advanced analytics and AI. As a result, compliance with the law is not sufficient to protect individuals or society from the threats that corporate use of these technologies can create. To protect people against these risks, and so to safeguard their own reputations and live by their values, companies need to do more than the law requires. As the interviewees described it, business "data ethics" management consists of the ways in which a company determines how far it wants to go beyond legal minimums, and how it seeks to achieve this goal. As a result, data ethics in the current period is largely a question of beyond compliance principles and assessments, even as legal norms continue to evolve. The literature has described such beyond compliance behavior with respect to corporate environmental performance. This Book documents beyond compliance behavior with respect to business governance of advanced analytics and AI.

**Keywords** Beyond compliance · Social license · Data ethics · AI ethics · Risk mitigation · AI sustainability

> **Key Take-Aways**
> - **Companies Need to Go Beyond Compliance to Protect Others, and so Themselves**: The law, including privacy law, lags the rapid development of advanced analytics and AI. As a result, compliance with the law is not sufficient to protect individuals or society from the threats that corporate use of these technologies can create. To protect people against these risks, companies need to do more than the law requires.
> - **Data Ethics Management is a Form of Beyond Compliance Behavior**: As companies themselves describe it, business "data ethics" management is a form of beyond compliance behavior that seeks to mitigate the risks that a

© The Author(s) 2024
D. Hirsch et al., *Business Data Ethics*,
SpringerBriefs in Law,
https://doi.org/10.1007/978-3-031-21491-2_4

company's use of advanced analytics and AI can create for individuals and the broader society, and so for the company itself.
- **Data Ethics Resembles Corporate Sustainability Efforts**: The literature has described such "beyond compliance" behavior with respect to corporate environmental performance. This Book documents beyond compliance behavior with respect to business governance of advanced analytics and AI.

Business use of advanced analytics produces benefits. But it also creates the harms outlined in the previous chapter. How can companies reduce or prevent these negative impacts? Where they do occur, how should businesses balance them against the positive outcomes? How should they determine whether a given advanced analytics project is legitimate and socially acceptable?

Traditionally, companies have looked to privacy law, and the Fair Information Practices (FIPs) that underlie them, as a guide in such matters. Privacy law generally requires that companies notify individuals before they collect and use their personal information, afford them some choice as to whether to allow this, and use the data only for the purpose specified in the notice and to which the individuals have acquiesced. So long as a company adheres to these core principles—notice, choice and purpose limitation—and the individual in question consents to the data processing, the company feels relatively comfortable that its data practices are legitimate. The individual consented to them, after all.

A number of interviewees explained that, while this approach may work for simpler forms of data processing, advanced analytics puts great strain on it. To begin with, the above-described harms that advanced analytics can impose extend well beyond privacy to bias, increased inequality, and other such areas. Privacy law's individual consent model is not designed to perceive and address these social harms. Second, U.S. privacy law governs only certain sectors, leaving important ones (social media, data brokerage, search engines, etc.) lightly regulated. Third, U.S. privacy law generally applies only where companies process personally identifiable information (PII). Advanced analytics, however, can find correlations in, and develop predictive algorithms from, de-identified information. Where companies de-identify data before analyzing it, they arguably take advanced analytics outside the scope of privacy law.[1]

Finally, the interviewees explained that, even if a company were to try to comply with the spirit of privacy law and the FIPs, the nature of advanced analytics makes this difficult to achieve. Companies that engage in advanced analytics typically start by compiling or gaining access to a massive dataset drawn from multiple sources. Later, they look for correlations in the data and, based on these patterns, make inferences and actionable predictions. As a result, the company carrying out the advanced analytics may be several steps removed from the entity that first collected the data. This makes

---

[1] As one interviewee put it: "[A]ll privacy laws in the world are written with the caveat of personal information. But if you think about the number of potential technology-enabled decisions or impacts an individual could be subject to that have nothing to do with personal information, you start to say: 'Well, wait a sec, that just doesn't work anymore....'" Interviewee #7.

it difficult to go back and obtain consent from the individuals whose data make up the data set. "[Y]ou may be so many steps removed, you can't possibly have gotten consent from the individual in way that is reflective of what you want to do with that data. So, I think that in of itself is a problem." (Interviewee #22).

Interviewees further explained that they often do not figure out what they are going to try to learn from the data—the purpose of their processing—until after they have amassed the data set. Thus, even where a company is involved in the data collection and so in a position to seek consent, it often cannot specify the purpose at the moment of data collection and can only obtain the most general kind of consent. As one interviewee put it: "[T]he problem is that in order for it to be meaningful consent, the person or organization who was seeking that consent at the time would had to have thought through every possible way those data could be used and at least to have framed up, at least at a generalized level, a consent that's actually broad enough in scope. They don't have the ability to do that, unless you say, 'You're consenting to everything that we possibly ever might want to do with this data.' It's problematic." (Interviewee #22).[2] Another concurred: "in the area of big data, where data is used well beyond the purpose of primary collection, it's almost impossible to get consent, informed consent, and consent that is useful." (Interviewee #23). For all of the above-described reasons, the interviewees believed that privacy law does not adequately address advanced analytics' potential harms, and that compliance with such laws is not a sufficient way to protect people from these harms.

The survey data shows something similar. In Fig. 4.1, we see that a clear majority of respondents said that current laws either do not address, or do not clearly and adequately address, the harm that advanced analytics can impose on individuals and the broader society. Some risks—such as lack of transparency, errors in decision-making, and especially displacement of workers through automation—were frequently rated as not addressed at all in current law. Other risks, such as privacy and manipulation, were seen as only ambiguously addressed in current law. Discrimination was the most likely of these risks to be seen as clearly addressed in existing law, and yet even here, more than 40% of respondents saw this legal treatment as ambiguous. While there is clearly a great deal of variation in legal clarity across different risks, these findings also suggest that companies must look beyond the law to address potential harms that they have identified as salient.

---

[2] Another interviewee made a similar point: "Let's put that in the context of big data. We have laws today that really are built on foundations of providing notice, providing a purpose specification, and gaining consent for whatever purpose you're specifying. That's simply inconsistent and does not take into account the reality of this observational world that we live in, or advanced algorithms where. . . the whole purpose of discovery is to discover causation or correlations that we can't anticipate. Otherwise, it's really just research, or analytics, which we've been doing for decades. The fact that we don't know what we're going to discover is simply inconsistent with specifying purpose". (Interviewee #21)

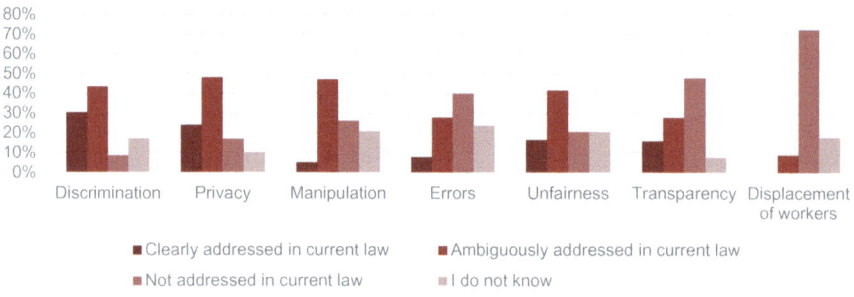

**Fig. 4.1** How well does current law address the risks from advanced analytics

Unable to rely on privacy law and individual consent as a source of legitimacy, some companies have begun to assess for themselves the social acceptability of particular advanced analytics projects.[3] They see themselves as venturing beyond privacy law and into the realm of substantive value choices, of ethics. For these companies, "data ethics" means assessing the legitimacy and acceptability of advanced analytics projects so that the company can act—or at least try to act—in a socially responsible way. "[T]he laws and regulations haven't caught up yet to this new, innovative use of data. Therefore, we will have to make our best guess at how to be ethical and responsible." (Interviewee #21).[4]

This shift from a consent-based model to substantive assessments of impacts and harms is reminiscent of the longstanding debate in the privacy law literature between individual control-based, and use- or harm-based, approaches to privacy regulation. What seems to be happening is that, when it comes to advanced analytics, some companies are starting to move on their own from a consent-based model, to a harm-based one. One interviewee spoke to this directly: "the FIPs were not created with this world in mind. Transparency and choice in a world that is opaque and complex are not going to solve all of these problems.... I think the conclusion of the White House report about looking at use-based rules in the complexities of this world was right. The difficulty of that is how do you do it?" (Interviewee #3).

Framed as beyond compliance management, data ethics shares much with other forms of corporate social responsibility, such as reducing carbon emissions, where companies go beyond compliance with the law. Data ethics is, in a sense, a form of corporate social responsibility for the algorithmic economy.

> I almost think that it comes down to just this perfect storm of the company's history and philosophy around social responsibility. Because I actually think that everything we're actually talking about here, ultimately, is social responsibility. Not unlike the labor issues; not

---

[3] As one interviewee put it: where "the ability to go and get consent, really meaningful consent, just doesn't exist, you need another basis on which to do what you're doing." (Interviewee #22).

[4] One interviewee directly tied the rise of data ethics to the reluctance to rely on consent: "[the] reason that the ethics conversation is important and interesting... is: when do ethics let me use data without consent?... I mean, could Google use all the searches and go play the stock market? Who knows what machine learning will enable them to predict? And what can Amazon do with the data it learns about my home?" Interviewee #19.

unlike the environment. I see patterns that are similar to the waves that we've seen of other social responsibility. And, I know we've never thought about this, or data protection, as a social responsibility function. But, I think ultimately it will be and those always align to the ethics department and tend to get pulled away from the legal department. (Interviewee #21)

We predict that, in the next five to ten years, growing numbers of U.S. companies will include data ethics as part of their general corporate social responsibility initiatives and reporting. We base this prediction on what we learned about the strong reasons for going beyond compliance to address data ethics risks. The next chapter sets out these reasons, as described by the companies themselves.

**Open Access** This chapter is licensed under the terms of the Creative Commons Attribution 4.0 International License (http://creativecommons.org/licenses/by/4.0/), which permits use, sharing, adaptation, distribution and reproduction in any medium or format, as long as you give appropriate credit to the original author(s) and the source, provide a link to the Creative Commons license and indicate if changes were made.

The images or other third party material in this chapter are included in the chapter's Creative Commons license, unless indicated otherwise in a credit line to the material. If material is not included in the chapter's Creative Commons license and your intended use is not permitted by statutory regulation or exceeds the permitted use, you will need to obtain permission directly from the copyright holder.

# Chapter 5
# Motivations—Why Do Companies Pursue Data Ethics?

**Abstract** This chapter examines the reasons that companies go beyond compliance to engage in data ethics management. Our research suggests that a range of different pressures and incentives may encourage companies to adopt data ethics policies. These include issues of corporate and industry reputation (particularly in the wake of scandals), emerging or looming regulation (in both the U.S. and other jurisdictions, especially the EU), demand from employees, and strategic interests in improving decision-making and gaining competitive advantages. Delving into reputational dynamics, the chapter considers the role of data ethics policies in gaining trust not only with consumers/users but also with regulators and business partners. Using our survey data, we examine how types of markets (business-to-business vs. business-to-consumer), media and stakeholder pressures, and perceptions of regulation may be related to whether companies have a data ethics policy or not.

**Keywords** Trust · Goodwill · Regulatory risk · Competitive advantage · Corporate values · Business ethics

---

**Key Take-Aways**

- **For the most part, businesses pursue data ethics management for strategic reasons.**
- **Companies pursue data ethics management for six main reasons:**
  1. **Build and sustain reputation and trust:** Companies worry that if they use advanced analytics and AI in ways that harm people or the broader society, this will damage their reputation with their customers, business partners and regulators. They invest in data ethics to protect the reputation and build trust with these important constituencies.
  2. **Prepare for and shape future law and policy:** Companies believe that regulation of advanced analytics and AI is coming. They undertake

beyond compliance activities to prepare for, or potentially pre-empt or influence, such regulation.
   3. **Recruit and retain employees**: Employees who perceive the company's data practices as harmful are more likely to leave, or not to accept a job offer in the first place. Better data ethics performance can enable companies to recruit and retain these employees.
   4. **Make faster and better decisions**: The uncertain risks of advanced analytics and AI projects can make it hard for companies to decide whether to undertake such projects. Standards and processes for assessing the social acceptability of an advanced analytics or AI project can enable businesses to resolve these issues more quickly and intelligently. In this way, effective data ethics management can facilitate faster and higher quality innovation.
   5. **Achieve competitive advantage**: Customers may prefer more ethical businesses and products. Companies seek to differentiate themselves and achieve greater market share by taking data ethics seriously.
   6. **Fulfill values**: Some respondents reported that it was their company's or CEO's deeply held values that motivated and informed its data ethics efforts. They see data ethics management as an extension of a broader commitment to corporate social responsibility.

- Survey data suggested that companies that faced external pressures from the media, advocacy groups, employees and/or investors for better data ethics performance were more likely to have a policy in place to manage the risks from their use of big data.

Chapter Four's account of data ethics as a form of beyond compliance risk mitigation leaves an important question unanswered: Why do companies make this effort? If existing U.S. privacy law does not require companies to be more responsible in their use of advanced analytics, why are they investing resources in doing so? Our research suggests that there is not a single driving factor but rather a range of different pressures and incentives that may encourage companies to adopt data ethics policies.

## 5.1 Build Reputation and Sustain Trust

For one thing, companies want to build and maintain their reputation and the trust that others have in them. Negative incidents involving advanced analytics, such as the Facebook-Cambridge Analytica episode, which was particularly salient among survey respondents, can erode this trust, damage reputation, and so hurt the business. Our interviewees frequently cited the need to maintain reputation and trust as among the most important reasons that they invested resources in identifying and seeking to reduce the threats that advanced analytics can pose.

## 5.1 Build Reputation and Sustain Trust

> Well, there's a lot of different people like me at other companies that are trying to ensure that the trust in their brand is maintained and extended and the trust in the marketplace because trust is the fundamental of all human relationships and that's why if you act ethically and ensure the data use is ethical and you are fully accountable for that, then your brand is trustworthy and I think that is the most important. That's what we're all trying to achieve, so there's many, many companies get it and are trying to stand up programs or extend programs that really get at this fundamental of trust and operating ethically. (Interviewee #6).

While legal compliance is necessary for building a strong reputation and trusted relationships, it is far from sufficient. Negative incidents that do not violate the law can still affect the public's perception of a company. For example, one interviewee pointed to the recent controversy in which ProPublica found that it was able to market ads to Facebook users who included the term "Jew Hater" in their profile.

> Well obviously, it's a big reputational issue for Facebook. They don't want to be viewed as a company that's serving up ads based on antisemitism, and likewise Google doesn't want to do that as well. So, it doesn't matter what the law requires. It's really a question of what's good for their business's reputation. And we run into that a lot with companies. (Interviewee #23).[1]

Companies that engage directly with consumers have the strongest incentive to avoid negative incidents and protect reputation and trust. For example, an interviewee from the retail industry explained that their company had developed a management approach to vetting advanced analytics that centered on whether the data practice would be seen as benefiting the consumer.

> After ascertaining that a given project complies with the law, the company then asks: "does it put the customer first, is it something we ought to do, is it brand right. . . . If we have a reputational hit and we have customers that either decrease spend or are not spending with us at all for whatever reasons, that's really something that we want to avoid. That's the harm, and that's the basis. But at the end of the day, it's really about the customer . . . does this put the customer first?". (Interviewee #17).

Other companies, particularly those that do not transact directly with consumers, focused on their standing with the general public. For example, one interviewee attributed their company's data ethics initiative to its decades-long reputation as "a really ethical company in the eyes of the public," and to the company's desire to maintain this reputation.

Other companies worried more about their reputation with regulators. As they saw it, legal compliance was not sufficient to maintain a good relationship with these public officials. They also needed to show that they were good actors. A high-profile incident involving the unethical use of advanced analytics could damage regulators' image of them, even if it did not involve a violation of law. The Facebook-Cambridge Analytica episode, which may or may not have involved a legal violation

---

[1] An attorney put it to their clients this way: "I can tell you this thing you're doing, that you're proposing, it's perfectly legal. But there's a really good chance there's going to be a really crappy New York Times article about you on this. I don't think you want that. So, let's brainstorm about ways that we can avoid that and achieve the business objective you're trying to achieve in a different way." (Interviewee #12).

but certainly caused regulators to scrutinize Facebook more carefully, illustrates this. As one interviewee explained:

> I think some of the companies are very motivated by wanting to . . . have good, trustworthy relationships with regulators. So they're seeking to balance a number of different factors: how regulators perceive them, how their customers perceive them as well as how actively they're able to use and move data around the world. (Interviewee #16).

One interviewee focused, not on customers or regulators, but on their company's reputation among its business partners. As this interviewee saw it, individual consumers lack the resources and expertise to assess meaningfully a company's data practices. Business partners, particularly those who share their data with a company, are much more likely to scrutinize these practices carefully, especially where a negative incident could reflect back on them. A company needs to handle data ethically in order to earn the trust of these business partners.

> As we all know, [individual] people don't read privacy policies. . . . When you're [a company that is] signing up for a CRM [customer relationship management] contract, for years and millions of dollars, you're reading every word of every agreement, right? . . . . Companies that sell these types of products need to make sure what they say in these contracts is true. But, more importantly that they're following their own controls and public statements about privacy and security protocols and living up to the values that they leverage when they sell these products. (Interviewee #9).

The survey data, however, suggests that reputation among business partners may not be a common driver of data ethics management, at least as compared to consumer-oriented reputations. As illustrated in Fig. 5.1, we found that companies in our sample that sell primarily to businesses are less likely to have a policy in place to manage the risks from advanced analytics and AI than do companies that sell primarily to consumers. Although this difference is not statistically significant (p = 0.21), the difference is certainly noticeable within the confines of our sample.

In sum, the interviews suggest that—whether to protect their standing with customers, regulators, business partners, or all three—companies pursue data ethics

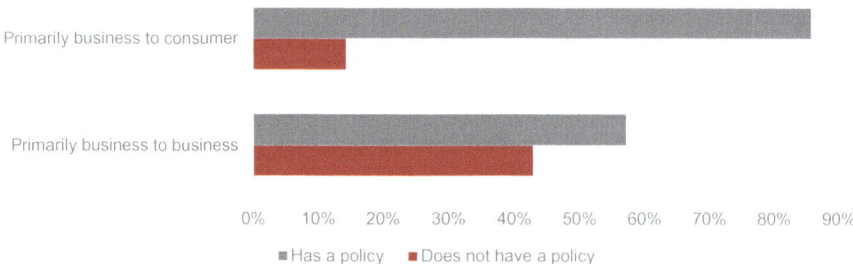

**Fig. 5.1** Incidence of company policy for managing risks of big data by whether a respondent's company is primarily business-to-consumer or business-to-business

5.1 Build Reputation and Sustain Trust

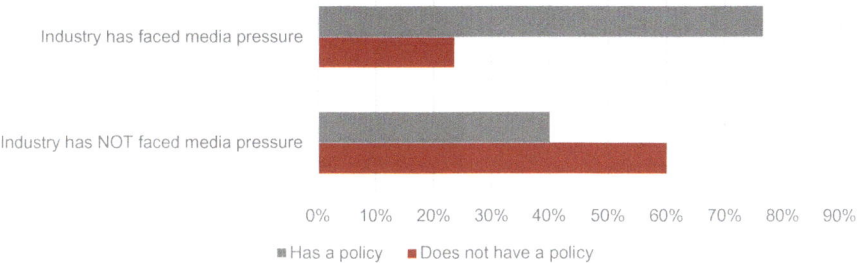

**Fig. 5.2** Incidence of company policy for managing risks of big data by whether respondent's industry has experienced media pressure

in part to protect their reputation as responsible stewards of people's data, even where the law does not require them to do so.[2]

> Preying on vulnerable populations, treating people unfairly, manipulating people in ways that could harm them . . . . There's some of that stuff that's perfectly legal, but it still may not be a good business decision. I'll throw out the word ethics. It's not the ethical thing to do. Some companies that I work with, they take that stuff very, very seriously. They don't want to do things that feel, or could be perceived as, unethical. (Interviewee #12)

The survey data supports the idea that trust and reputation are important drivers of corporate data ethics management. For example, in addition to asking survey respondents whether their company had adopted a policy for managing the risks of big data, we also asked respondents whether the media (Fig. 5.2), advocacy groups (Fig. 5.3) or employees or investors (Fig. 5.4) had brought pressure on companies in their industry to achieve better data ethics performance. As conveyed in the following figures, companies were more likely to have a policy for managing big data's risks when their industry had experienced such pressures. While these findings are not statistically significant, the direction of associations is informative. Collectively, Figs. 5.2, 5.3 and 5.4 suggest a link between external pressures and having a policy in place to manage the risks from big data. Perhaps most notably, more than 75% of companies in industries that faced media exposés, investigative journalism, or media criticism related to data ethics had a voluntary policy, compared to only 40% in industries that had not faced this kind of scrutiny.

While the current survey was designed as exploratory and does not seek to assess causality, we did look further into the timing of media pressures and the creation of policies. Approximately 50% of respondents indicated that the media pressures on their industry began in 2015–2019 (rather than in earlier periods), and almost 75% of these companies adopted their policies between 2016 and 2019. The overlap

---

[2] One interviewee explained that their company derives great value from its reputation and that this justifies an investment in data ethics. "A company kind of built their reputation over a 25-year period. And it's worth billions of dollars as an asset. And so they're very protective of that. And so... they are willing to devote substantial resources in making sure that they avoid [things that detract from their reputation." Interviewee #15.

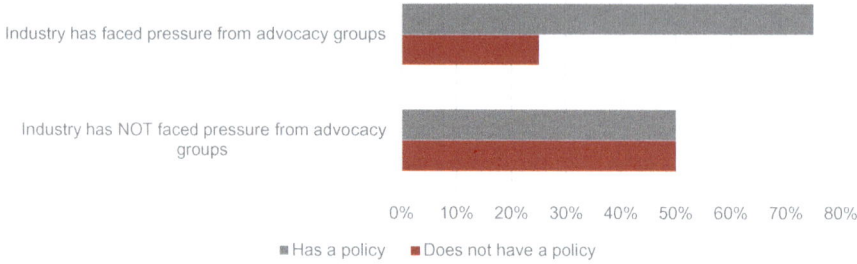

**Fig. 5.3** Incidence of company policy for managing risks of big data by whether respondent's industry has experienced pressure from advocacy groups

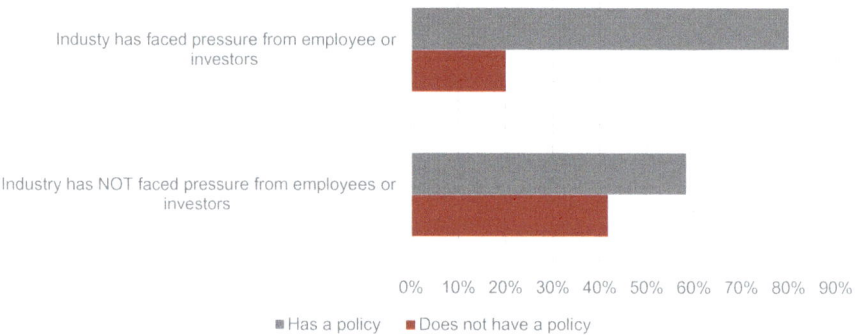

**Fig. 5.4** Incidence of company policy for managing risks of big data by whether respondent's industry has experienced pressure from employees or investors

of periods suggests that external pressures and data ethics policies tended to grow together in tandem in a relatively short period of time, as opposed to one greatly preceding the other. This provides a baseline for future research into the more precise timing of public pressures, media coverage, and the development of company policies.

## 5.2 Anticipate Emerging Regulation

Companies generally put resources into curbing externalities because laws require them to do so. At the time of the data collection for this book (2017–2019), US law did not directly require organizations to weigh the benefits and risks that their use of advanced analytics and AI could create. American companies that processed European's personal data did have to comply with Article 22 of the European Union's General Data Protection Regulation (GDPR) which expressly regulates "automated decision-making." But Article 22 required merely that organizations include a human in the decision-making loop. It hardly mandated they undertake data ethics management.[3]

Instead, the interviewees explained that it was the likelihood of *future* regulation that motivated their companies to invest in data ethics management. At the time of the interviews, the Facebook-Cambridge Analytica story, which involved Cambridge Analytica's use of advanced analytics to manipulate voters,[4] was fresh news and was sparking interest in federal privacy legislation. Congress was considering a number of privacy bills, some of which would have curtailed abusive big data analytics practices (Kerry 2019). At the same time, the Federal Trade Commission suggested that it might use its Section 5 unfairness authority to reign in algorithms that had disparate, negative impacts on racial minorities or other protected classes.[5]

Due to developments such as these, the interviewees believed that the future regulation of advanced analytics and AI was likely. The survey respondents shared this view, although they were a bit less certain on this point than the interviewees. We asked the survey respondents whether they agreed—from 1 (strongly disagree) to 5 (strongly agree)—that there would be new US Federal or State government regulation of big data analytics in the coming years. As conveyed below in Fig. 5.5, almost 70% of the sample agreed that some state regulation was likely, while almost 50% agreed that federal regulation was likely.

With the benefit of hindsight, we can now see that the interviewees and survey respondents were right about how the law was likely to develop. In the years since we collected our data, the European Union has proposed, and will very likely soon pass, the AI Act. (Commission, EU 2021) In the US Senate alone, Senator Wyden has introduced the Algorithmic Accountability Act (US Cong., Senate 2022), Senator Coons the Algorithmic Fairness Act of 2020 (US Cong., Senate 2020), and Majority Leader

---

[3] Insofar as the GDPR had any impact on U.S.-based businesses' pursuit of data ethics, it was likely due, not to Article 22, but to Article 6 titled "Lawfulness of Processing." Where an organization is unable to secure data subject consent—as is often the case when it comes to advanced analytics—Article 6 allows it to process personal data if the organization's "legitimate interests" in processing the data outweigh the data subject's "fundamental rights and freedoms." By getting companies to articulate and balance benefits and the risks, Article 6 likely made a greater contribution to data ethics than Article 22. (Interviewee # 22). The GDPR's most important contribution to corporate data ethics may have stemmed from its legitimate interests balancing test. As one interviewee put it, "there is not a lot of difference between the type of analysis you do, to make sure that the score card is balanced for what legitimate interest, and what you would do to make sure that benefits and risks are balanced in big data." (Interviewee #1).

[4] Cambridge Analytica obtained the data of 87 million Facebook users. Using advanced analytics, it inferred the personality types of these individuals. It then sent them political ads, at the behest of the Trump campaign, that appealed to each voter's particular personality type and so influenced them in ways that they could not consciously detect. Cambridge Analytica's use of advanced analytics, and its potential impact on the Presidential election, is one of the reasons that this incident outraged so many people.

[5] Federal Trade Commission, *Big Data: A Tool for Inclusion or Exclusion?* 23 (January 2016) (stating that "Section 5 may also apply . . . if products are sold to customers that use the products for discriminatory purposes. The inquiry will be fact-specific, and in every case, the test will be whether the company is offering or using big data analytics in a deceptive or unfair way.")

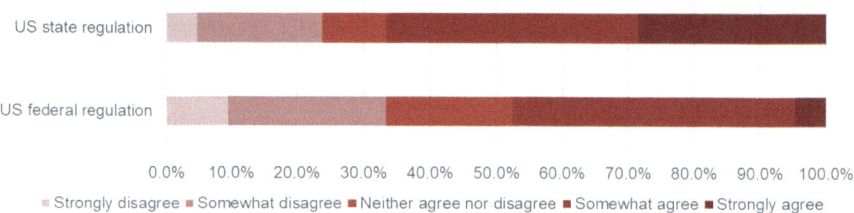

**Fig. 5.5** Do you agree with the statement that there will be new regulation (federal or state) of big data analytics in the next 5 years

Shumer has promised an "all-hands-on-deck effort in the Senate, with committees developing bipartisan legislation, and a bipartisan gang of non-committee chairs working to further develop the Senate's policy response" to AI. The bi-partisan American Data Privacy and Protection Act, the leading federal privacy bill, contains a provision (Section 207) devoted exclusively to "Civil Rights and Algorithms." State and local governments have actually *passed* legislation that directly regulates advanced analytics and AI. Notable examples include a Colorado statute to prohibit unfair algorithmic discrimination in the insurance industry, and a New York City law requiring independent audits for algorithmic bias before employers can use algorithmic decision-making in their hiring processes. The survey respondents were right, not only about the likelihood of future regulation, but about the fact that state regulation was likely to precede federal action (see Fig. 5.5).

At the time of data collection these legislative proposals and actions were still in the future. But companies' anticipation of them formed a second, major motivation for engaging in "beyond compliance" data ethics management. The interviewees explained that their companies hoped, through these actions, to achieve one or more of three objectives. To begin with, some companies believed that if industry could demonstrate that it understood and was able to reign in advanced analytics' harmful aspects, that might render unnecessary and prevent the passage of stringent government regulation. As one interviewee who worked with a variety of businesses on their data ethics initiatives explained:

> a business with smarts, they would be advocating for self-regulatory or even co-regulatory types of models that held them accountable to a different standard of accountability or stewardship as a means to stave off what will invariably be badly written [regulation that will] have negative consequences from a data perspective to businesses. (Interviewee #7).

A second group of companies focused not so much on pre-empting future regulation as on shaping it. They worried that ill-informed government regulation could be incompatible with their business models and operations. They believed that, if they took the initiative to develop and implement strategies for reducing advanced analytics' harms, policymakers might draw on these models when drafting legislation and regulations. That could make future regulation both more effective and more feasible from a business perspective.

## 5.3 Recruit and Retain Employees

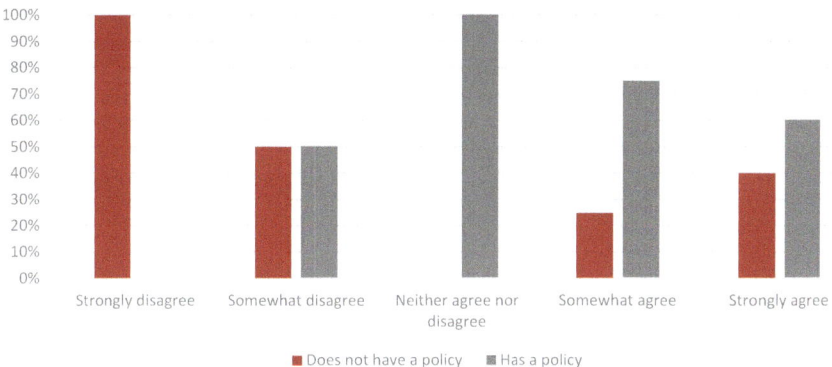

**Fig. 5.6** "Do you agree with the statement that there will be new state regulation of big data analytics in the next 5 years," by whether a company has a policy in place

But the smart ones are going to say wait a sec, this is the inevitable future and I want to stay at least one step ahead of it. And they're going to start to both work to influence the development of those regulatory guidance frameworks and ... to implement their own ethical or fair data processing standards as a means to achieving sort of trusted data optimization. (Interviewee #7).

Finally, there were companies that wanted to get ahead of future regulation so that, when it did come, they could adapt to it more easily, and at lesser cost, than their competitors. These "smart organizations are seeing the tea leaves and saying, 'I really want to make sure that I stay at least one step ahead of that.'"(Interviewee #7). These three motivations—to pre-empt, shape and prepare for future regulation—were important drivers of corporate investment in responsible advanced analytics and AI. Still, the move in this direction remained more the exception than the rule. "[F]or many organizations, they just don't want to invest in something unless they have to."(Interviewee #7). In our survey, we see a positive association between having a policy in place to address the risks of advanced analytics, and the extent to which respondents see US state regulation in the near future (Fig. 5.6).

## 5.3 Recruit and Retain Employees

Several interviewees linked data ethics to employee retention. This was particularly evident among firms that employed data scientists. At the time of our research, these individuals were in very high demand. They were more likely to move to another employer when the company for which they worked used data in ways that offended their values. A pro-active approach to data ethics thus became important to employee retention which, itself, was critical to the company's success.

> I will say one thing about engineering companies in the Valley . . . the engineers themselves –these 24-year-old kids – are powerful. . . . They are valuable and they are the strength of the company. So, . . . there's two markets you compete in for a tech company: one is to sell your products, the other is to attract talent – the talent market. If you don't get the best talent, you don't have the best product. . . . [T]hese are engineers coming out of generally elite, progressive, generally liberal institutions. They're going to come in with sort of a mindset that is very pro-privacy and civil liberties. They want to do the right thing. (Interview #10).

## 5.4 Make Faster and Better Risk-Based Decisions

It may sound counter-intuitive, but the driving force for some companies to limit their use of advanced analytics was their desire to use advanced analytics more fully. This stemmed from companies' uncertainty over the line between socially acceptable and unacceptable uses of this technology. Faced with this uncertainty, many companies found it difficult to make risk-based decisions about particular advanced analytics use cases. Risk-averse companies then held off on such uses, and so lost out on the value that advanced analytics, as applied to their data, could have generated.[6] Companies that put resources into data ethics management and so developed a way to spot and navigate ethical issues connected to their use of advanced analytics not only protected people better, but also improved their ability to make quick and effective decisions about whether to proceed with particular analytics projects. This freed them up to use advanced analytics, and their own data, more fully. One consultant who worked with many companies, referred to this as overcoming "reticence risk."

> [Q]uite frankly, . . . the biggest driver of data value creation loss, and the increasing problem organizations face, is what I call self-inflicted reticence risk. It is their inability to make internal decisions about whether they should or shouldn't do something related to the use of data. . . . In the absence of a decision-making process inside the company, the risk voices always win. The result is these organizations end up leaving value on the table. . . . The decision-making process should address: 'I don't know whether I can use data;' and, 'even if I legally can do it, I don't know whether I should do it.' Absent a more formalized decision-making process, organizations find that many, if not every, stakeholder inside the company has an opinion on this and that and these opinions cannot be reconciled. The result is that data activity grinds to a halt . . . and these organizations end up only using only 30%, 40% of the data or the value because they can't reconcile the risk. . . . Reticence risk is leaving value on the table because you just can't make a risk-based decision. (Interviewee #7).

---

[6] One study estimated that the median Fortune 1000 company could increase its revenue by $2.01 billion a year just by marginally improving the usability of the data already at its disposal. Anitesh Barua, Deepa Mani, and Rajiv Mukherjee. "Measuring the Business Impacts of Effective Data," University of Texas McCombs School of Business, September 1, 2010, p. 3.

## 5.5 Achieve Competitive Advantage

A surprisingly large number of interviewees said that their companies pursued data ethics for competitive advantage. In a sentiment related to the above comments on reputation and trust, some focused on the market benefits of a good reputation.

> [I]f you get people to believe . . . that you are handling things in a responsible manner, they're more likely to keep doing business with you or want to do business with you. . . . It can help you in the marketplace. . . [Anytime] we are able to talk about how we are handling or managing data in a responsible way, it does nothing but help our brand and our reputation. (Interviewee #9)

Others framed the advantage differently. As they saw it, an ethical product or project is one that benefits, rather than harms, customers. They believed that, by proactively working to prevent harm to consumers, they would improve the customer experience and so make the company's products more attractive.

> [I]t's also . . . what's the customer experience? It's just making them think through things that I wouldn't have had a problem with. They're not necessarily data ethics concerns. But suddenly they'll just realize this is actually to have a crappy customer experience. . . . So they're actually seeing this as a benefit from the business perspective. (Interviewee #20).

This is also how they explained their role to the business units that they worked with. They found this message to be more effective than an explicitly ethics-based one.

> If you go to a team and say, "Hey, I'm here to do ethics review." They immediately think, "What? Am I being unethical? Am I doing something wrong?" . . . It sends the wrong message. So I often frame ethics questions as product improvement questions. Like, "I just want to know how you're doing things, and let me see if I can help you figure out what the sensitivities might be, and how we can resolve them." And those questions then, are ethics questions. And that's really my job right now. . . So, that's what we're doing here, is we're making these projects better because we ask questions. . . . we have many, many examples where we are truly proud of the work that we did as a team, because we know that we improved the project. (Interviewee #14).

A 2016 Price Waterhouse Coopers report suggested a number of levels on which data ethics could create competitive advantage, maintaining that "[t]hose that [have more developed ethical frameworks] could find themselves a magnet for employees, customers, and even investors who increasingly favor organizations that operate ethically and responsibly. In fact, several studies have confirmed that companies operating ethically outperform others in revenue and profitability . . . [they] gain a strategic advantage by excelling in leveraging data's upside while managing risk and reducing costs." (PwC 2016). One data ethics manager expressed a similar sentiment: "the time has come . . . where privacy is a differentiator, and data ethics is even something that's going to further differentiate . . . I don't think there's any way you can escape it." (Interviewee #16).

Data ethics managers likely have a vested interest in believing that their work makes their company more competitive and successful. These same managers may not be the most reliable reporters on whether, in fact, data ethics management has this effect. Based only on these reports, we cannot conclude as to whether data ethics does, in fact, produce such an advantage. But we can report that some data ethics managers see themselves, and explain their role to their companies, in this way.

## 5.6 Fulfill Corporate Values

The above motivations behind data ethics management are rooted, in one way or another, in the company's self-interest. However, a number of the interviewees felt strongly that their companies pursued data ethics for more intrinsic reasons having to do with the company's core values. As one said:

> [T]hat's not the only driver, following the rules, following the law. I think [my company] has other drivers. One is company values. Those might extend beyond the exact letter of the law, and I think [company] is a values-based company, and I'm not just saying this as a marketing pitch, this is what I think. I think [company] has strong values about protecting its customers, protecting its own information, and its employees, and then making sure that it's a good steward of public information. [The company] puts a lot of energy and puts forth a lot of resources to be a good steward in those regards. (Interviewee #18).

The above, anecdotal account of the motivations behind data ethics management does not allow us to say which motivations are most important. But it does suggest that there are many reasons why a business might put resources into data ethics management, even when the law does not yet require it to do so. That explains why some companies might engage in beyond compliance data ethics management. But it does not yet tell us *how* they do so. What does data ethics management look like in practice? What are its main features? What challenges does it encounter? Chapters 6–10 share what we learned about how organizations pursue data ethics management.

## References

Commission, EU. 2021. Laying down harmonised rules on artificial intelligence (artificial intelligence act) and amending certain union legislative acts. Proposal for a regulation of the European parliament and of the council. COM (2021) 206 final.

Kerry, Cameron. 2019. *Breaking Down Proposals for Privacy Legislation: How Do They Regulate?* Brookings (March 8, 2019).

PwC. 2016. *Responsibly Leveraging Data in the Marketplace: Key Elements of a Leading Approach to Data Use Governance.*

United States Senate. 2020. Algorithmic Fairness Act of 2020. Congress.gov, https://www.congress.gov/bill/116th-congress/senate-bill/5052. 116th Congress, Senate Bill 5052, introduced 17 December 2020. Accessed August 8, 2023.

United States Senate. 2022. Algorithmic Accountability Act of 2022. Congress.gov, https://www.congress.gov/bill/117th-congress/senate-bill/3572. 117th Congress, Senate Bill 3572, introduced 3 February 2022. Accessed August 8, 2023.

**Open Access** This chapter is licensed under the terms of the Creative Commons Attribution 4.0 International License (http://creativecommons.org/licenses/by/4.0/), which permits use, sharing, adaptation, distribution and reproduction in any medium or format, as long as you give appropriate credit to the original author(s) and the source, provide a link to the Creative Commons license and indicate if changes were made.

The images or other third party material in this chapter are included in the chapter's Creative Commons license, unless indicated otherwise in a credit line to the material. If material is not included in the chapter's Creative Commons license and your intended use is not permitted by statutory regulation or exceeds the permitted use, you will need to obtain permission directly from the copyright holder.

# Chapter 6
# Drawing Substantive Lines

**Abstract** This chapter discusses the benchmarks and standards companies use to distinguish between ethical and unethical uses of advanced analytics and AI. In recent years scholars, governmental bodies, multi-stakeholder groups, industry think tanks, and even individual companies have issued model sets of data ethics and AI ethics principles. These model principles provide an initial reference point for setting substantive standards. However, the breath and ambiguity of these principles, and the conflicts among them, make it difficult for companies to operationalize them in all-things-considered decisions. In our study, most companies accordingly grounded their data ethics decisions, not on abstract ethical principles, but on intuitive benchmarks such as the Golden Rule or what "feels right." Such gut-level standards, while potentially useful for approximating public expectations, are difficult to teach or apply consistently. Companies need substantive standards that are more actionable than high-level principles, and more standardized than intuitive judgment calls. They need generalizable *policies* that draw the line between ethical and unethical applications of advanced analytics and AI. How best to generate such company-specific policies remains an open question. One company said they did this by capturing past data ethics decisions and using them as "precedents" to guide future such decisions.

**Keywords** Substantive standards · AI ethics · Ethical principles · AI principles · Golden rule

> **Key Take-Aways**
> 
> - **Substantive standards are vital**: Organizations that want to use advanced analytics and AI ethically need substantive standards that enable them to draw the line between ethical, and unethical, applications of this powerful set of technologies.
> - **Formal ethical principles are abundant, but hard to operationalize**: The many sets of data ethics principles published in recent years provide an initial

reference point for setting substantive standards. However, the breath and ambiguity of these principles, and the conflicts among them, make it difficult for companies to operationalize them in all-things-considered decisions.
- **Most companies rely on informal and intuitive benchmarks**: At the time of our study, most companies grounded their data ethics decisions, not on formal ethical principles, but on intuitive benchmarks like the Golden Rule or what "feels right."
- **Policies are needed**: Data ethics policies that are prospective and standardized and, at the same time, provide specific guidance on how to resolve data ethics issues, are useful. However, at the time of our study, companies were only beginning to formulate and implement them.

Having looked at why companies are pursuing data ethics, we turn now to *how* they are doing so. The interviews suggest that business data ethics management programs consist of two, main components: (1) technical measures for making the company's advanced analytics and AI systems fairer, more privacy protective, and more explainable; and (2) management standards, structures, and processes for making difficult data ethics judgment calls. The interviewees provided some information about technical measures and Chap. 9 reports on what we learned about this key component of data ethics management.

The interviewees and survey respondents were, for the most part, data ethics managers, not technologists. They accordingly focused on the second core component of data ethics management: the standards, structures and processes required to make difficult data ethics judgment calls. Advanced analytics and AI are powerful tools that have outpaced the law's ability to regulate them. Companies can accordingly use these technologies for purposes that, while technically legal, may still hurt or offend people. For example, a company might use advanced analytics to infer that a person has a high risk of heart disease and decide, on this basis, not to issue a loan to them. Or, it may infer that a person is suffering from mental health problems and so market mental health services to them. Each of these applications could increase the company's profits. But are they the right thing to do? And if customers or the media learn about them what will this mean for the company's reputation? Some refer to these as ethical issues. Others call them the 'should we' questions—shorthand for 'we can do it technically, and we can do it legally, but should we?' The interviewees focused on how they, and their companies, make these often-difficult ethical judgment calls. This book, too, focuses on this second, core component of data ethics management.

How do companies spot and decide hard data ethics issues? After reviewing and synthesizing the twenty-three interviews, we identified three, core steps that most of the businesses seemed to share: (1) creating substantive standards that the company could employ to draw lines between ethical, and unethical, uses of advanced analytics and AI; (2) establishing management structures to assign and allocate responsibility for the data ethics function; and (3) instituting management processes to spot and

## 6.1 Published Data Ethics Principles

resolve data ethics issues and so to keep the business on the "ethical" side of the substantive lines that it has drawn. This chapter focuses on the first of these steps, the drawing of substantive lines. Chapter 7 discusses data ethics management structures and functions, and Chap. 8 focuses on the management processes that businesses use for spotting and resolving difficult data ethics issues. Chapter 9 will describe some of the technical measures that companies employ to make their use of advanced analytics and AI fairer, more privacy protective, and more explainable.

### 6.1 Published Data Ethics Principles

To resolve a data ethics issue, an organization must be able to draw a line between uses of advanced analytics and AI that are ethical, and those that are not. Once it has done so, it can then determine whether the project or application in question falls on one side of this line or the other. The first step in developing an effective data ethics management is accordingly to adopt the substantive standards that define which uses of advanced analytics and AI are ethical, and which are not.

In recent years, an extensive body of literature has discussed AI ethics principles. Scholars, governmental bodies, multi-stakeholder groups, industry think tanks, and even individual companies have contributed to this literature. These works largely follow a similar pattern. The author first sets out an ethical framework grounded in human rights, a school of philosophy, bioethics, fiduciary duties or some other established set of principles. The author then suggests that organizations use these principles as the basis for distinguishing between ethical and unethical advanced analytics and AI practices.

In the scholarly arena, Floridi and Cowls (2019) illustrate this approach in their article titled *Unified Framework of Five Principles for AI in Society*. Floridi and Cowls maintain that data ethics shares much in common with bioethics.[1] They set out a unified framework for data ethics that adopts the key principles of bioethics— *beneficence, non-maleficence, autonomy*, and *justice*[2]—as well as one additional principle, *explicability*. They maintain that these "Five Principles for AI in Society" should guide specific sectors and industries as they decide which AI practices are ethical and which are not.

On the governmental front, the European Data Protection Supervisor's Ethics Advisory Group's (EAG) 2018 report, "Towards Digital Ethics,"[3] offers its own list of guiding principles. These include Dignity, Freedom, Autonomy, Solidarity, Equality, Democracy, Justice and Trust (European Data Protection Supervisor 2018).

---

[1] *Id.*

[2] The first four of these principles emerge from the dominant approach to bioethics and medical ethics (Beauchamp and Childress 2013).

[3] Governmental bodies in the European Union have led the way in in articulating data ethics guidelines and principles. As in the realm of privacy regulation more generally, other countries will likely follow the Europeans' lead. It is therefore useful to consider examples of how EU governmental bodies contribute to the data ethics literature.

The Ethics Advisory Group put forth this set of principles so that companies and others engaged in advanced analytics could "integrate [them] in both their designs and business planning reflection about the impact that new technologies will have on society."[4]

A year-long multi-stakeholder process involving policymakers, industry stakeholders, civil society organizations, and professional orders, among others, produced the Montreal Declaration. The Declaration identifies ten principles to guide the use of artificial intelligence: (1) Well-being, (2) Respect for autonomy, (3) Protection of privacy and intimacy, (4) Solidarity among people and generations; (5) Democratic participation, (6) Equity, (7) Diversity inclusion, both social and cultural, (8) Prudence in anticipating potential adverse consequences, (9) Human responsibility, and (10) Sustainable development.[5] It establishes these principles as a guide for private and public entities to use in developing and deploying AI in ways that "are compatible with the protection and fulfilment of fundamental human capacities and goals."

Industry-oriented think tanks and trade associations articulate similar sets of principles to guide corporate use of advanced analytics. For example, the Information Accountability Foundation, an influential industry-funded think tank based in the US, published a Unified Ethical Frame for Big Data Analysis. (Information Accountability Foundation 2015). This document recommends that, in "developing an assessment framework necessary to assure a balanced, ethical approach to big data," companies should seek to align their advanced analytics practices with five core values: "Beneficial, Progressive, Sustainable, Respectful and Fair."

Finally, a growing number of companies have begun to adopt and publish their own sets of data ethics or AI ethics principles. For example, Google's Objectives for AI Applications states that AI should: "1. Be socially beneficial; 2. Avoid creating or reinforcing unfair bias; 3. Be built and tested for safety; 4. Be accountable to people. 5. Incorporate privacy by design principles. 6. Uphold high standards of scientific excellence."[6] Microsoft's AI Principles are quite similar: (1) Fairness. All systems should treat people fairly (2) Reliability and Safety. All systems should perform reliably and safely (3) Privacy and Security. All systems should be secure and protect privacy (4) Inclusiveness. AI systems should empower everyone and engage people (5) Transparency. AI systems should be understandable (6) Accountable. People should be accountable for AI systems.[7]

These examples are just a slice of a much broader array of articles, reports and statements that set out abstract ethical principles to guide the deployment of advanced analytics and AI. In a 2020 report, Harvard University's Berkman Klein

---

[4] EDPS 2018 at 7. *See also, id.* at 15 (describing the principles "as a means to fill critical gaps in existing legal regulations and as a way of supporting those actors who work to adapt ethical principles to rapidly evolving issues, which often outpace the evolution of law.").

[5] https://nouvelles.umontreal.ca/en/article/2018/12/04/developing-ai-in-A-responsible-way/ (accessed 8 August 2023).

[6] https://ai.google/principles/ (accessed 8 August 2023).

[7] https://www.microsoft.com/en-us/ai/responsible-ai?activetab=pivot1%3aprimaryr6 (accessed 8 August 2023).

## 6.1 Published Data Ethics Principles

Center for Internet and Society identified and analyzed several dozen such frameworks from government, civil society, the private sector, multi-stakeholder groups and inter-governmental organizations (Fjeld et al. 2020). The report identified eight core themes that many of them share: privacy, accountability, safety and security, transparency and explainability, fairness and non-discrimination, human control of technology, professional responsibility, and promotion of human values. Jobim et al. (2019) analyzed 84 sets of AI ethics principles and identified eleven overarching themes.

Rather than consolidating all sets of principles into a single framework, as the Berkman Klein Center did in its report, we find it helpful to distinguish between two categories of such frameworks which we call "moral" and "practical." On the one hand are frameworks that appear to be grounded in moral philosophy or human rights traditions. The EU Data Protection Supervisor's Ethics Advisory Group's focus on "Dignity, Freedom, Autonomy, Solidarity, Equality, Democracy, Justice and Trust,"[8] and the Montreal Declaration,[9] with its emphasis on "well-being," "solidarity," "autonomy" and "equity," exemplify the "moral" category. They integrate moral and human rights ideals that are at once so universal and essential that they are almost beyond question, and so abstract that, unless they are further elaborated, would prove difficult for a company to operationalize. By contrast, Google's Objectives for AI Applications[10] emphasizes practices—such as accountability, privacy by design, avoiding unfair bias, building and testing for safety—that are grounded in traditions of privacy management and practice. They appear more practical and implementable, even as they leave out essential moral and human rights commitments that might drive a company towards something more worthy of the term "ethics" (note that Google refers to "objectives," not "ethics.").

Figures 6.1 and 6.2 show that a substantial percentage of the survey respondents were aware of, and influenced by, these ethical frameworks. In particular, Fig. 6.2 shows that many respondents had seen specific documents produced by organizations like the Information Accountability Foundation and Future of Privacy Forum. While this would suggest that published external principles are important, it is not clear from the survey just how influential these types of ethical principles are. In fact, most interviewees stated that their companies resorted to informal benchmarks (discussed below) to make decisions rather than formal, ordered sets of ethical principles. One key issue is that, although the lists of principles may inform discussions within companies, in and of themselves they frequently do not lead to an all-things-considered judgment of *what to do*.

---

[8] *Id.* at 16–21.

[9] https://nouvelles.umontreal.ca/en/article/2018/12/04/developing-ai-in-a-responsible-way/ (accessed 8 August 2023).

[10] https://ai.google/principles/ (accessed 8 August 2023).

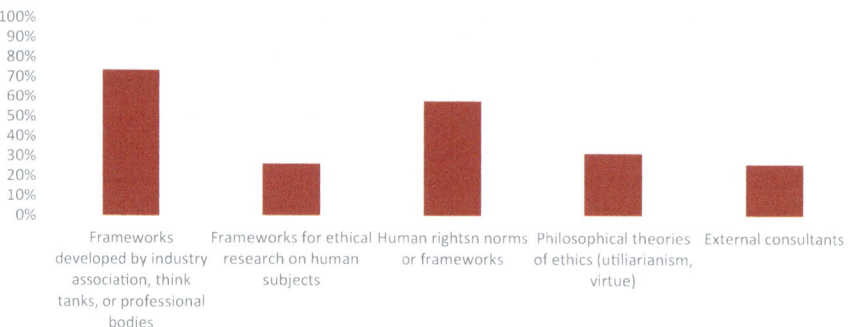

**Fig. 6.1** Did any of the following shape the content of your internal policy for dealing with the ethical risks of big data analytics?

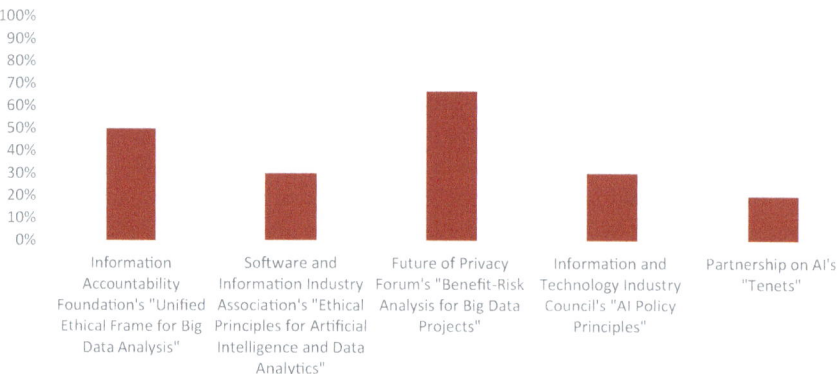

**Fig. 6.2** Has anyone within your company to your knowledge seen any of these documents?

## 6.2 Informal Standards

Given the abundance of relevant ethical principles, and the survey responses indicating that many in our sample were familiar with such principles, our research team expected the interviewees to state that their companies were using such substantive frameworks in their ethical decision-making. But that is not what we found. Fourteen of our interviewees were corporate employees (the other nine worked for law firms, think tanks, or were consultants that advised companies on data ethics matters). Of the fourteen who worked for companies, only three referred to formal principles when explaining how their companies made data ethics decisions. We describe their accounts below. The remaining eleven companies described their companies' heavy reliance on informal benchmarks for making these decisions. The ethics lead for a large tech company explained that their approach was "heavily leaning [towards] the informal [approach to data ethics decision-making]. We don't have any: 'Hey, based

## 6.2 Informal Standards

on this document that we wrote six months ago, this is now sensitive, or meets that qualification, or meets the definition of risky." (Interviewee #14).

The survey data on professional training of those who handle the data ethics function is consistent with the interviewees' reliance on informal benchmarks rather than formal ethical frameworks or sets of principles. The survey asked whether the respondents' "work has been influenced by any type of formal ethics training." Of the twenty-two survey recipients who responded to this question, only one indicated that they had a formal degree in ethics, and only six said that they had received ethics training of any type from a source outside the company. By contrast, twelve of the twenty-two said that they had a law degree. This suggests that those charged with making data ethics decisions are unlikely to have deep knowledge of ethical frameworks or philosophies. They are more likely to have received training in the kind of practical judgements, informed by laws and by broad human rights or ethical concepts, that lawyers tend to make.

The interviewees were very clear about applying informal standards. For example, a privacy professional at a leading technology company explained that, when presented with a sensitive or highly innovative project, they first apply a cursory "ear test." Only if the project passes the ear test does it get sent on for full Review Board consideration. The ear test is highly informal.

> The ear test simply means to me: does that sound right, does that sound like a bad idea? Do the words coming out of your mouth make sense from a legal, ethical, and business standpoint?" . . . [W]e really think of those as kind of cursory, baseline ethics analysis. Our attorneys ask themselves: 'does that feel right what you're saying, what you're suggesting? You want to use this data for this purpose . . . . Does that make sense? . . . does that just feel right? (Interviewee #18).

Another highly experienced privacy officer at a major company described employing a "fairness check." The executive described this as: "Would my mother think this is okay? Would I want this to happen to my kid? Do I feel good about this personally?... We all know unfairness when we see it and I think that's an important construct and you'll hear it. It's a resonant term. Everybody in the policy circles is beginning to talk about, 'Is it fair to the individual?" (Interviewee #6). A third interviewee explained that "the standards we use are primarily two things: One, are you finding this creepy? Which is an undefined, but everybody knows it means, standard – the creepy standard. Two, do you want to live in the world that this creates?" (Interviewee #10).

Creepiness. The "ear test." What would my mother think? Do I want to live in the world that this data practice creates? These are informal, intuitive, expectation-based judgements, not formal ethical principles. Most of the companies that we spoke with were using standards of this type to draw the substantive lines between ethical, and unethical, uses of advanced analytics. Two central ideas permeate this informal approach. One is desire to stay within the expectations of important stakeholders.[11]

---

[11] Where companies went beyond customer expectations, they tried to do so gradually and carefully. "You can't flip that overnight . . . . You've got to put in some work here to bring the customers, bring the consumers, bring the regulators, bring everybody that might be looking at this in concern

One privacy officer explained that they ask engineers: "do you really think grandma's expectation was that her data was going to be used in the way you're suggesting when she allowed for it to be collected?" (Interviewee #18). Another, talking about the informal test that their company applies, recounted that "[t]here's one person in the company that calls it the newspaper test. There's another person that has the grandmother test. There's all these metaphors that are used when these kinds of things are decided. If we're going to end up telling an individual and sitting down with them for an hour to explain exactly what we're going to do, if there's any chance that that person would object to that, then the general rule is, then we shouldn't do it." (Interviewee #21).

The second theme is the Golden Rule—"Do unto others as you would have them do unto you." When privacy professionals pose the question: "do you want to live in the world that this creates," (Interviewee #10), or "[w]ould I want this to happen to my kid?" (Interviewee #6), they are, in a sense, asking their engineering teams and organizations to follow the Golden Rule. Abstract ethical frameworks may help one to think about these questions. But ultimately, as one experienced attorney told us, it comes down to "more of a gut feel, to be honest." (Interviewee #12). That is what we found companies to be doing. They are making ethical judgments based on whether the practice in question "feels right" after considering stakeholder expectations and the Golden Rule.

How to understand this? Given the abundance of available ethical principles, why are these leading companies instead going with what "feels right"? The interviews suggested a number of reasons. To begin with, abstract principles such as "justice," "autonomy," "freedom" and "solidarity"—those that one finds in the Montreal Declaration, EU Ethics Advisory Group report, and other frameworks that we have put in the "moral" category—are too general and subject to interpretation to serve as effective guides to decision-making. They are more likely to tangle decision-makers in debates than lead them to an efficient resolution. As one privacy leader put it: "I don't want to turn everybody into a pointy headed philosopher, and we wouldn't get anywhere, right? That was a little bit of a concern when we first started talking about this internally, was that we would get into some kind of analysis paralysis, we'd never move things along, and things would always get stuck in data governance.... We want to keep things moving, right? Innovation doesn't mean we just sit here." (Interviewee #16). The informal standards that companies use—public expectations, the Golden Rule—are themselves open to interpretation. But people can more readily apply these standards based on their own experience. "What would *I* expect?" "How would *I* want to be treated?" That is a way of framing the question that can produce a relatively quick and useful resolution, even if not a philosophically grounded one. Informal standards are thus more practical than abstract ethical principles.

Informal standards are also more accessible to corporate employees who frequently lack formal training in philosophy or ethics. "If you say, 'Hey, have some

---

along, so they can understand what's happening and why it's happening, and what consumers are getting back from this. So that a conversation can take place and we can develop a new norm." (Interviewee #12).

ethical thoughts,' they're not going to know what that means because they are not ethically trained. So that's when you say, 'Hey, just think about the 'what if' questions. Like, what if this project does this? And what if this project actually does not do this for that population? Is that fair?' You're putting ethics questions into their heads without telling them they're ethics. And that's the trick." (Interviewee #14).

Informal standards also align well with the purposes behind corporate data ethics initiatives, which may be the main reason that companies adopt them. As was discussed above, most companies view data ethics as a form of beyond compliance risk mitigation. They pursue it in order to be seen as trustworthy and responsible, and so to protect their reputations and reduce the threat of regulation. Conforming to people's and regulators' expectations, and living by the Golden Rule, are ways to show that one is responsible and trustworthy. Informal, expectation-based standards thus align with, and serve the purpose behind, data ethics initiatives. Public-facing, broad statements of principle also connote trustworthiness and responsibility. That may be why companies adopt them while, at the same time, relying on more informal standards for the actual decision-making.

The key challenge for such an approach is drawing the line between acceptable and unacceptable risk. Because responsible decision-making in the beyond compliance domain requires sensitivity to, and balancing and weighing of, a wide range of ethical risks, even the risk management approach cannot avoid consulting substantive principles, public expectations, the Golden Rule, intuitive "feel", or some other standard in order to guide judgments.

## 6.3 Risk Management Frameworks

A few data ethics managers and consultants embraced the risk mitigation function more expressly. They framed data ethics as a form of risk management. "I think the path through this is, we'll call it ethical, call it responsible, call it fair, whatever word it is, it's being able to design and implement responsible data practices that include an impact assessment on individuals or, quite frankly, a risk assessment as to the individual, as the receiver of that risk." (Interviewee #7).

Generally, risk management is defined as the identification, evaluation, and prioritization of risks followed by an economical application of resources to minimize those risks (Hubbard 2009). The interviewees expanded on this basic concept in two ways. First, they emphasized the importance of considering the *benefits* of a given advanced analytics and AI project, in addition to its risks, and then of balancing the two. As one explained, "the risk management tools that I implement with organizations do benefits, minus inherent risks [reduced by controls] . . . to get at a net benefit risk score."(Interviewee #7). This approach is reminiscent of the Future of Privacy Forum's (FPF) 2014 Report, *Benefit-Risk Analysis for Big Data Projects* (Polonetsky et al. 2014). In that report the FPF, a privacy think tank largely supported by contributions from its corporate members, emphasized the importance of considering a project's benefits along with its risks. It suggested that companies first identify the benefits of a given advanced analytics and AI project; then evaluate the project's risks; then consider how to mitigate these risks; and, finally, balance the benefits against the mitigated risks. If the mitigated risks outweigh the benefits, drop the project. If the benefits were greater than the mitigated risks, proceed.

Second, the interviewees stressed the importance of considering impacts, not only on the company and its customers, but on a much broader array of stakeholders. "I would say it starts with first thinking about the actual individuals that are affected by the decisions you make.... That is not necessarily part of the mindset when people are just thinking about compliance.... Whereas an ethical approach is much more centered on who's affected by this, what are the risks, and what are the harms, but what also are the benefits...? So, it's a weighing of what I'll call risks and harms and benefits and the different stakeholders." Data ethics, particularly when framed as risk management, gets the company to think about impacts on stakeholders that it might not otherwise have considered.

Only a few of our interviewees expressly mentioned the risk management approach. Given the close alignment between risk management and the risk mitigation goal behind corporate data ethics initiatives, we expect to see more companies adopt this approach to substantive line drawing and begin to build the risks of engaging in advanced analytics into their broader risk management efforts.

## 6.4 Formal Principles in Action

As was mentioned above, three of the fourteen corporate interviewees said that their company had established a formal set of principles to guide their use of advanced analytics and AI. One privacy manager at a major health care company was quite explicit about the need to move beyond informal judgment calls to principle-based decisions.

> [When] we look at things through an ethical lens, we really do try to apply a principled approach.... I'm in the stages right now of drafting our code of data ethics for the organization, because people do need to see... they need to see some enumerated framework, right? When we go into our data governance meetings, what does that mean, right? [W]e provide, again, principles of ethics to consider, as opposed to just saying, "Does this feel right? Does it not feel right?" I think that's where ethics sometimes gets stuck, because folks don't know how to think ethically, and I don't mean that in a disparaging way. It's not to say we can't be moral thinkers, but what does that mean in terms of data?(Interviewee #16).

When we dig deeper into this interviewee's approach, however, we see that even they combine these formal principles with more intuitive, user-friendly standards. The interviewee starts from "health care ethics... autonomy, beneficence, nonmaleficence, and justice" but recognizes that "[t]hat's not going to mean much to a data scientist." (Interviewee #16). The interviewee then translates these principles into "questions that you might want to ask yourself."(Interviewee #16).

> [T[he principle of autonomy... [w]e've reshaped that a bit to say that when we look at data, we need to continually remind ourselves that there is a human being behind this data....

## 6.4 Formal Principles in Action

> there is a respect for the person who is behind that data.... We use the principle of empathy, which is to say, "Let's put ourselves in the shoes of our customers." If you're looking at length-of-stay reports, for example . . . [i]t isn't enough to say they should not be there more than three [days]. We need to look at what are the consequences.... when we're looking at drawing inferences from data. So we use the principle of empathy.... gathering as much ... data as you can about this person and apply principles of empathy to it. 'Is it right?' 'Do you feel right about what you're doing?' We've used that principle as well. (Interviewee #16)

This interviewee begins by making the case for enumerated principles and explaining that informal standards such as "does this feel right" are insufficient, but then goes on to explain that, in fact, they rely on such an informal standard. In operationalizing the principles of autonomy, beneficence, etc., the interviewee first translates them into "empathy" and ultimately invokes "Do you feel right about what you're doing?" Even where there is a desire for enumerated principles, the practical value of informal, intuitive standards asserts itself.

In another example, an interviewee reported that their Silicon Valley company had articulated a set of ethical principles to guide its data practices. "It's pretty basic. It talks about... privacy and civil liberties but other things as well, and it has a few basic things like we would never be involved in supporting work that might repress a democratic group,... or that represses speech." (Interviewee #10). As with the interviewee from the health care industry, this interviewee almost immediately transitioned into talking about how difficult it can be to operationalize these formal constructions. For example, the interviewee posed the question of whether working with law enforcement in Europe to investigate and prosecute hate speech would count as "working for a group that represses speech?" (Interviewee #10). The interviewee went on to explain how the company had tried to translate its set of principles into a re-usable set of questions for ethical decision-making but had to abandon the project after the still-growing list of questions reached thirty-four pages in length.

> We tried to break it down into a reusable framework of questions and we worked with our advisors to do this, to figure out what questions do we need to ask, what framework do we need to use and we stopped at 34 pages of questions. Because we just realized trying to capture it all in advance wasn't working. Trying to create these redlines in advance, again incredibly difficult. (Interviewee #10)

This account of the difficulty that a company experienced in trying to turn broad principles into usable interrogatories supports the idea, stated above, that companies adopt informal benchmarks because formal ethical principles do not lend themselves to practical decision-making.

Some companies do use high-level rules in a way that seems to work. They identify a set of data-related actions that the company believes to be harmful, and then steer clear of these "no go" areas. For example, one retailer refused to accept customer ethnic codes from third parties (Interviewee #17). A number of companies that collect personal data for marketing purposes (customer data, web surfing data, search data) decided not to sell it to third parties who might use it for other purposes (Interviewees #17, 19). Some companies decide that, while they will sell data to other commercial entities, they will not sell it to the government.[12] Others, who collect customer data for advertising purposes, decide that they will not use it for other, secondary purposes. While these are bright line rules about specific situations, rather than the type of broad concepts (autonomy, equality, etc.) that one finds in the sets of data ethics principles discussed above, their use suggests that principles can inform a company's sense of what not to do, even if they do not easily result in a judgment of what *to* do.

If broad data ethics principles do not lend themselves to practical decision-making, then why are companies adopting them? They may serve a hortatory purpose by setting aspirational goals that inspire employees to think more seriously about data ethics and that communicate to the public that the company takes its data ethics responsibilities seriously. They also play an important role in issue spotting. As one interviewee explained:

> But I think that the big value [of data ethics principles] is to direct people's attention to issues. There's issue spotting. . . . Given people's backgrounds and interests and expertise, you may be tempted to think narrowly in what you're doing, just in terms of achieving the short-term business goals. And what these principles do, especially if they're made part of corporate culture, is to say I know your job is to come up with ideas that cause more engagement among our members . . . . but here's some other things that you should do at the same time. That's where these principles can do some good. (Interviewee #15)

## 6.5 Policy: The Missing Middle Layer

There is a third alternative that lies between broad, abstract principles and intuitive, expectation-based judgments: corporate policy. Policy can be prescribed from the top. But it can also emerge in a common law fashion when managers, confronted with a difficult question, take broad principles, interpret and apply them based on common sense and "what feels right," and so produce a decision. If captured and compiled, those decisions constitute a growing set of corporate policy in much the same way that judicial decisions create common law, or administrative adjudications produce agency policy.

The interviews showed a glimmer of such policy development. An interviewee from the pharmaceutical industry and one from the health care industry each explained that their company captures and stores its data ethics decisions and then makes them available as a type of precedent for future decision-making. Over time, such a process should yield a corpus of policy guidance that is far more functional

---

[12] "A company I talked to a year ago had been approached by the intelligence community for its mobile ad data, it sells this data to its clients, I don't know why the intelligence community wanted it but they said, 'we think this is a really bad idea right?' and I said, 'yeah, it's a really bad idea, it is legal, and they may be able to go get it from your client, but you should not sell it to them, that's going to be viewed as unethical by your customers who don't believe that because they saw your ad or they saw a pixel that the government should have it.' So that's a place where people are drawing clear lines." Interviewee #19.

## 6.5 Policy: The Missing Middle Layer

than broad, hortatory principles, and more consistent and unified than case-by-case judgments grounded in gut feeling and ever-changing public expectations.

The interviewee from the pharmaceutical industry explained that their company maintains a set of rules to govern data-related actions, including the use of advanced analytics. An employee who wants to initiate a new project must consult these rules and, where the rules are ambiguous or do not speak to the question, the employee must then consult with a member of the team who is trained to answer such grey area questions. The decision then gets recorded and becomes part of the set of rules that guide future decisions. "[O]nce guidance is provided, it automatically loops back and gets instantiated . . . . It's like case law." (Interviewee #21). The interviewee from the health care industry explained that, once the company has built up such a set of precedents, they speed up the review process. "[S]o there's more, what I will call precedents, to go off of. If something looks like the one we just looked at in July, [then] you can [follow the precedent and] keep it moving." (Interviewee #16).

An interviewee from a Silicon Valley-based technology company provided a very different picture, describing "ad hoc" decision-making that does not draw on prior precedents:

> And so that means every time you get this ad hoc decision-making it runs huge risks . . . . [A]re we building a common law here? I don't think we are because we don't necessarily record, . . . I'm not sure we record the nuanced decisions in a way that lets us say "okay, how did we do this in the past." We obviously have a lot of churn, it's a tech company, obviously everybody's young, people start their own business, stuff like that. The institutional knowledge – at [number less than 10] years I'm one of the more senior people at the company now – the institutional knowledge isn't necessarily there. It creates a ton of challenges, how do you actually do this in a meaningful way that you can repeat?". (Interviewee #10)

This anecdotal evidence suggests that companies in highly regulated, long-standing industries such as pharmaceuticals or health care may have existing organizational structures for making, capturing, and compiling policy precedents that they are utilizing with respect to advanced analytics and data ethics. Newer, Silicon Valley-type companies, which lack these institutional structures and, perhaps, need to move more quickly, may struggle more with policy development in this area. Precedent-based policy, which is both practical and consistent, appears to bridge the gap between impractical aspirational principles and ad hoc intuitive judgments. We expect more companies to produce this middle layer of data ethics policy as the field matures.

Whatever the strategic motivations of the companies in this study, it seems clear to both the participants and the research team that there is no way to build a reputation for the responsible use of people's data without entering thoughtfully into the world of beyond compliance data ethics. Our examination of the interviews and survey results revealed an important distinction that shapes our analysis, namely, the distinction between (1) ethical standards or principles that define particular wrongs (or harms or risks) and (2) standards that define what constitutes responsible decision-making by a company. Any comprehensive, beyond compliance business data ethics approach will need to offer companies not just an enumeration of substantive ethical principles and their associated harms or risks, but a separate standard or procedure that tells them how to weigh and apply those principles to reflect their moral or social responsibilities in uncertain terrain. Appreciating this distinction ties specific data-related ethical concerns to long-standing debates about corporate obligations in society and draws attention to the need for effective structures and processes within a company that will allow them to track and meet those obligations. We turn to those now.

## References

Beauchamp, T., and J. Childress. 2013. *Principles of Biomedical Ethics*, 7th ed. New York: Oxford University Press.
European Data Protection Supervisor's Ethics Advisory Committee. 2018. Towards Digital Ethics.
Fjeld, Jessica, Nele Achten, Hannah Hilligoss, Adam Nagy, and Madhulika Srikumar. 2020. *Principled Artificial Intelligence: Mapping Consensus in Ethical and Rights-Based Approaches to Principles for AI*.
Floridi, Luciano, and Josh Cowls. 2019. A unified framework of five principles for AI in society. *Harvard Data Science Review* 1 (1): 1–15.
Hubbard, Douglas. 2009. *The Failure of Risk Management: Why It's Broken and How to Fix It*.
Information Accountability Foundation. 2015. Unified Ethical Frame for Big Data Analysis.
Jobin, Anna, Marcello Ienca, and Effy Vayena. 2019. The global landscape of AI ethics guidelines. *Nature Machine Intelligence* 1: 389–399.
Polonetsky, Jules, Omer Tene, and Joseph Jerome. 2014. Benefit-Risk Analysis for Big Data Projects. https://fpf.org/blog/big-data-a-benefit-and-risk-analysis/. Accessed August 8, 2023.

**Open Access** This chapter is licensed under the terms of the Creative Commons Attribution 4.0 International License (http://creativecommons.org/licenses/by/4.0/), which permits use, sharing, adaptation, distribution and reproduction in any medium or format, as long as you give appropriate credit to the original author(s) and the source, provide a link to the Creative Commons license and indicate if changes were made.

The images or other third party material in this chapter are included in the chapter's Creative Commons license, unless indicated otherwise in a credit line to the material. If material is not included in the chapter's Creative Commons license and your intended use is not permitted by statutory regulation or exceeds the permitted use, you will need to obtain permission directly from the copyright holder.

# Chapter 7
# Management Structures and Functions

**Abstract** This chapter discusses the organizational challenges that businesses face when they pursue data ethics management and the development, in response to these challenges, of new organizational roles and structures to manage data ethics. The nature of data ethics management requires organizations to move away from traditional compliance or quality control check modes and towards prevention of ethically problematic actions. Some organizations have proactively begun to develop new organizational roles and structures that can help standardize data ethics management practices. New roles, such as the Data Ethics Officer, have emerged, as have new entities such as the Data or AI Ethics Committee. These new positions and committees make difficult data ethics decisions and translate new knowledge about data ethics into organizational practices. After introducing these new structures and functions, we discuss the importance of role clarity (i.e., who is responsible for data ethics) within organizations and its relationship with developing organizational structure to support data ethics management.

**Keyword** Data ethics management · Data ethics officer · AI ethics officer · AI ethics committee

> **Key Take-Aways**
>
> - **Management is essential**. Drawing substantive lines between ethical, and unethical, uses of AI is only the first step. The organization must also manage its operations to ensure that it stays within these boundaries. This includes making a particular person and/or committee responsible and accountable for the data ethics management function.
> - **New management functions and structures are needed**. The data ethics management function goes beyond the privacy one. It addresses bias, manipulation, opacity and other risks that go well beyond privacy violations. And it aims towards a beyond compliance goal rather than compliance with

privacy regulations. Given this, data ethics management requires organizations either to expand the privacy role, or to establish new positions and entities capable of managing the data ethics function.
- **Organizational location varies.** Organizations made different choices as to where to house the data ethics officer or committee. Some companies chose to locate the data ethics function in their privacy unit since it has traditionally handled externalities associated with use of personal data. Others locate it in the legal unit, or elsewhere in the organization.
- **Data ethics officers and committees play important roles.** Some organizations localize the data ethics management function in a data ethics officer—a position that was only just emerging at the time of our research—or expand the privacy officer position to encompass it. Some create an internal, cross-functional data ethics committee. In a company that has both a data ethics officer and an AI ethics committee, the two may share responsibility for establishing policies and procedures and for making data ethics judgment calls, with the committee usually deciding the highest stakes issues.
- **The data ethics function tends to be a strategic, rather than a compliance-oriented, one.** Privacy management focuses primarily on compliance with privacy laws. By contrast, data ethics management goes beyond compliance with existing laws in order to build and sustain trust and prepare for future regulation. This is a strategic, rather than a compliance-oriented, function. In some companies, the strategy unit was the one that pushed for data ethics management.

It is not enough to draw substantive lines. A company must also manage its operations to ensure that it abides by the lines that it has drawn. The interviewees spent the bulk of their time describing the management practices that their companies use to try to achieve this. These practices break down into three main areas: organizational structure, processes for spotting data ethics issues, and processes for deciding those issues. This chapter describes the emerging structures for data ethics management. Chapter 8 describes the processes for spotting and deciding data ethics issues.

## 7.1 Organizational Structures

An organization that wants to accomplish something must generally localize responsibility for achieving the objective in a person or group that can then be held accountable. In setting up a data ethics management operation, one of the first things that the companies we spoke to needed to decide was who within the organization should "own" this area, and where should they sit within the company as a whole. Who should be responsible for data ethics?

## 7.1.1 Privacy Office

The majority of the companies that we spoke to assigned this function to a Chief Privacy Officer or some other privacy manager. The interviews suggest the thinking behind this. For some time now, the main risks associated with personal information have been privacy harms. When companies that use advanced analytics and AI confront new threats from their uses of personal data—bias, manipulation, etc.—they take them to the privacy office. As one interviewee explained about the privacy team that they lead: "We've become the de facto ethics team. We're the people that people come to with far more than just privacy questions, so we end up being a conduit for that.... they say 'alright well, these are the sorts of questions this team does, we'll take it to them.'" (Interviewee #10). Statements like this suggest that the companies allocated this role to the Chief Privacy Officer and privacy team more by default than by design.

## 7.1.2 Legal Department

Another common choice was the legal or compliance office, units that may, or may not, encompass the privacy function.[1] One interviewee explained that the Legal Department is generally responsible for doing due diligence on uses of data throughout the company. This gives it representation throughout the company and so enables it to spot and process data ethics issues wherever they arise (Interviewee #19). A second interviewee drew a distinction between the Legal and Compliance Departments and explained that Legal was preferable for the data ethics function because it is accustomed to making risk-based judgments under conditions of uncertainty, whereas Compliance is more used to bright-line rules.

> My area reports up through the law department, which is interesting, because when I originally assumed this role, it was part of compliance . . . It made sense to move under legal, we also wanted to get out of the checkbox kind of compliance thinking. When you think of compliance, you think, "I check the box and I take care of what I need to do." . . . [T]hat's really . . . not the appropriate way we want our folks to think about it. (Interviewee #16)

The survey data suggests that, in most companies, either the legal department or the privacy office (which may, in some companies, be part of Legal), has primary responsibility for managing the ethical issues that the company's use of advanced analytics may create. We asked respondents: "Who in your company has primary responsibility for managing ethical risks associated with big data analytics?" Table 7.1 displays these results and indicates that the Chief Privacy Officer or a Legal executive have primary ownership for the ethical risks. We asked a follow-up about this person's background and learned that over 50% of the specific individuals charged with managing ethical risks have a legal or compliance background.

---

[1] In the survey, 18.5% of respondents indicated that the Legal or Compliance Offices housed the data ethics function.

**Table 7.1** Who in your company has primary responsibility for managing ethical risks associated with big data analytics?

|  | Percent |
|---|---|
| No one in particular | 10.7 |
| Privacy officer or similar | 32.1 |
| Legal or compliance executive or manager | 32.1 |
| Other high-level officer (e.g., Chief Data Officer) | 3.6 |
| Data ethics officer or similar | 14.3 |
| Other | 7.1 |

**Table 7.2** Does your company have a Chief Data Ethics Officer?

|  | Percent |
|---|---|
| No | 82.8 |
| Yes | 17.2 |

**Table 7.3** Does your company have a Chief Privacy Officer?

|  | Percent |
|---|---|
| No | 10.3 |
| Yes | 89.7 |

### 7.1.3 The Chief Data Ethics Officer

An interesting development was the emergence during the interview period (2017–2019) of a new executive position related to advanced analytics and customer trust, the Chief Data Ethics Officer,[2] and, in some organizations, the creation of an Office of Data Ethics. In some companies, this function was combined with the privacy one. In others, it was distinct. As the time that we performed this research, the Data Ethics Officer role was still quite rare. Companies that had made a significant commitment to data ethics management made up our entire interview sample and, due to selection bias, were likely over-represented in our survey sample as well. Yet only one in five companies in the interview sample had recently created a data ethics officer or similar position, and only 17% of those in the survey sample had done so (Table 7.2). By contrast, almost ninety percent of survey respondents indicated that their company had a Chief *Privacy* Officer (Table 7.3).

The Chief Data Ethics Officer role goes well beyond that of the typical Chief Privacy Officer. To begin with, the Data Ethics Officer is responsible for all data about humans that could harm people, not just personally identifiable information (PII). A Chief Privacy Officer, by contrast, generally focuses on PII. As one former chief privacy officer explained:

---

[2] One company refers to it as the "AI Ethics," rather than "data ethics," function, and makes a group of people, rather than a single individual, responsible for it. Interviewee #2.

## 7.1 Organizational Structures

> I've just changed the name of the global program and my title has officially changed. My official title is now [title that includes "Data Ethics"] and I've changed the name of the global program to [name that includes "Data Ethics."] And it is because the way that we've done it at [company] is full accountability of all the data that we process and that we steward. That's a very different thing than ensuring you of just privacy requirements like notice and choice. [The idea that the company] should be comprehensively accountable for the data collection, the data activation, the data transformation, the data distribution, is a very next-generation program. It's always been built on ethics. We've been talking about the program as ethical data use for about five years. Then I, as I say, a few weeks ago, I made the official change. That's our journey. (Interviewee #6)

The data ethics function also goes beyond privacy to encompass responsibility for other advanced analytics and AI-related risks such as bias, manipulation, labor displacement and many of the other threats described above.

While privacy officers tend to focus on compliance with privacy laws, the data ethics function must focus on beyond compliance solutions since the law generally does not yet address the threats that advanced analytics can pose. One such professional explained that at the beginning of their tenure the CEO said to her: "I want compliance out of your title. This is not about compliance. This is about customer trust. Let's figure out a new title. So that's the birth of the title." (Interviewee #20). Another expressed a similar evolution:

> We actually added data ethics last year, so my title and my department changed. . . . if we are to do what we need to do for our customers . . . [w]e need to get folks to think of what privacy means a little differently, that it isn't simply complying with the law or policies, it is looking at things through an ethical lens. Because much of what we're doing with data is . . . in a space that is not occupied by law. . . . [D]ata ethics is getting a primary spot. That's the name of our department now. (Interviewee #16)

### *7.1.4 The Data Ethics Committee*

Another important management innovation was the creation of a new entity, the data ethics committee. These bodies could craft the organization's data ethics strategy, set data ethics policy, and decide or make recommendations on the highest stakes and most difficult data ethics issues.

These functions required multiple types of expertise and perspectives, and companies generally designed the committees as cross-functional entities that bridged a number of departments. The precise make-up varied from company to company but generally included representatives from the legal, privacy, security, communications, data analytics and engineering departments, as well as the affected business unit (Interviewees #6, 14). Some included individuals from government affairs (Interviewee #19), or from corporate social responsibility, (Interviewee #2). The committee might also seek input from C-Suite executives, including the CEO.

Data ethics committees, while growing in popularity, remained a minority approach at the time of our 2019 survey. Even in the survey sample, which likely over-represented companies that took data ethics seriously, only 33% of the respondents used such a committee for formal review of data ethics concerns. Over 40% of

**Table 7.4** What is your company's process for identifying ethical risks?

|  | Percent |
| --- | --- |
| We do not have a process set up currently | 18.5 |
| Informal screening or review–by a person or office (such as a data ethics executive or team) | 22.2 |
| Formal screening or review–by a person or office (such as a data ethics executive or team) | 11.1 |
| Formal screening or review by an internal committee, advisory board, or specialized body (e.g., ethics committee, IRB, etc.) | 33.3 |
| Screening or review of another sort | 11.1 |
| I do not know | 3.7 |

respondents indicated that their company had only an informal review process, or no process at all (see Table 7.4 for full distribution of companies' processes). We expect the use of data ethics committees to increase as a growing number of companies confront the risks that their use of advanced analytics can create.

### 7.1.5 Philosophers in the Corporate Ranks

Another personnel-related innovation was the hiring of PhD philosophers onto the privacy and data ethics team. One interviewee, explaining the role that the philosopher plays in their groups, discussed the debate that the company had as to whether to create encrypted communications that the government could not access:

> [A]t the heart of that is the question, what is the consequences of that, and even that, why do we have government? What is the purpose of government and what happens if we change the fundamental way the world operates by creating this extra-governmental space and is that good or bad . . . . And so being able to think through those questions and recognize those questions is a big part of what we do. Lawyers . . . our job is to look at the legal implications; engineers' tunnel vision is: "I want something that works fast and effectively," and so philosophers are helpful in dragging us out of those mindsets and thinking about, looking at the broader implications. It's an incredibly valuable insight. And we're employing philosophers, which has got to be valuable. (Interviewee #10)

This comment suggests that the data ethics team's need to consider broadly the social implications of advanced information technologies has led to the integration of philosophers trained to think rigorously about such matters.

### 7.1.6 From Compliance to Strategy

The growth of data ethics management, as personified by the Chief Data Ethics Officer and the Data Ethics Committee, may signify a fundamental change in the

## 7.1 Organizational Structures

way that companies manage data-related risks. The interviewees explained that, traditionally, the Privacy Officer's role was to make sure that the company complied with governing privacy laws. This made the Privacy Officer a type of internal cop, and the privacy function a drag on the business operation, even if a very necessary one.

Data ethics, by contrast, is not about compliance. It is about going *beyond* compliance with existing legal requirements to mitigate risk and maintain the company's reputation as a good steward of people's data. It seeks to build the trust that stakeholders (customers, users, business partners, regulators, and the general public) have in the company. This makes data ethics management similar to other business units—those focused on quality and reliability, communications, or customer relations—whose ultimate goal is to build and preserve the company's trusted relationships with customers, regulators and other important stakeholders. While corporate staff have tended to view the privacy function as a box that the business units need to check, they are increasingly coming to appreciate the data ethics as contributing to the core business mission of building trust and goodwill. If privacy was a compliance function, then, increasingly, data ethics is a *strategic* activity. One interviewee who had made the change from privacy officer to data ethics officer spoke about the transition in just this way:

> [The shift from privacy officer to ethics officer] is reflective of a really different way of approaching the subject . . . [R]eframing the whole discussion around customer trust has transformed the way I'm able to talk to the business. Before . . . the goal was to simply to get it by me, to check the compliance function. . . . [Then] I went in and I said, hey, this is about whether our customers trust us. . . . So that was the lens that the business understood. They understood how important it is to keep customer trust. They want more customers. So when I talked to them about the customer experience and customer trust, it completely turned it around. . . . The reality is we're ending up going so much farther and building things that are far superior in terms of the customers' experience around privacy. Just because I started with how the business wants to design products and services. (Interviewee #20)

Another interviewee whose position had grown from privacy to data ethics explained the distinction in strikingly similar terms: "Privacy became more of an operational function for the organization.... we became an enterprise solution." (Interviewee #16). One interviewee told us that it was neither the compliance, privacy nor legal offices that pushed for the establishment of a data ethics function; it was the *strategy office*. "They were the ones that saw the need for it and created it." (Interviewee #2). The fact that, in this case at least, the impetus for data ethics management sprung from the strategy group further suggests the changing role of data risk governance from a legal or compliance function to one linked much more closely to enterprise strategy. We anticipate that, in the years to come, more companies will create structures for data ethics management and that they will do so largely for strategic reasons such as those outlined above in Chap. 5.

**Open Access** This chapter is licensed under the terms of the Creative Commons Attribution 4.0 International License (http://creativecommons.org/licenses/by/4.0/), which permits use, sharing, adaptation, distribution and reproduction in any medium or format, as long as you give appropriate credit to the original author(s) and the source, provide a link to the Creative Commons license and indicate if changes were made.

The images or other third party material in this chapter are included in the chapter's Creative Commons license, unless indicated otherwise in a credit line to the material. If material is not included in the chapter's Creative Commons license and your intended use is not permitted by statutory regulation or exceeds the permitted use, you will need to obtain permission directly from the copyright holder.

# Chapter 8
# Management Processes

**Abstract** Management processes are essential to an organization's ability to spot and address ethical issues. In this chapter we investigate the types of processes used by organizations to manage ethical risks related to their use of advanced analytics and AI. We find that it is typical for organizations to develop processes for spotting ethical issues, escalating them to the appropriate decision-maker, and for reaching decisions about these issues. There is no single "silver bullet" approach to these vital data ethics management tasks and we saw a variety of practices. Some organizations placed data ethics professionals at various parts of the organization to spot ethical issues and escalate them to the center. Others employed checklists for data scientists, or consultation with external advisors. For decision-making, some organizations deployed a cross-functional data ethics committee. The committees at some companies operated with more autonomy and authority than those at others. We conclude this chapter by discussing how organizations can go beyond their traditional boundaries and institute processes that govern, not only the company's own use of advanced analytics and AI, but also that of their suppliers and customers.

**Keywords** Issue spotting · Ethical decision-making · Responsible AI · Checklists · AI governance · Data governance

> **Key Take-Aways**
> - **Data ethics management processes can be grouped into two categories**: processes for spotting and escalating data ethics issues, and processes for reaching decisions about these issues.
> - **Organizations use a number of different processes for spotting data ethics issues**. These include a "hub and spokes" approach that places ethics

professionals in the business units where they can spot issues and escalate them to the center; an external advisory group that sensitizes the organization to risks it might not otherwise perceive; and checklists that encourage engineers to consider and avoid actions that can lead to ethical issues; regular meetings at which employees discuss data ethics issues; and peer-to-peer discussions with data ethics managers from other organizations.
- **Organizations that prioritize speed tend to localize data ethics decision-making in an individual; those that prioritize deliberation tend to localize it in the cross-functional data ethics committee.** Our research suggests that Silicon Valley-type companies that prioritize speed to market tend to vest data ethics decision-making authority in one individual who may have a direct line of communication with the C-Suite or CEO. By contrast, companies in more traditional sectors seem to rely on a cross-functional data ethics committee that, while slower, is able to provide multiple perspectives and reach a more considered, and perhaps higher quality, decision.
- **Data ethics committees follow different decision-making models.** Some require consensus, while others follow a majority rule. Some have the power to make final decisions and even stop proposed projects, while others offer recommendations to the business units but do not hold the final decision-making authority. A company's culture and management style will likely determine which approach it prefers.
- **Data ethics management programs vary in scope.** Some focus only on the company's own use of advanced analytics and AI, while others take a more systemic approach that encompasses suppliers and customers.

Putting the right structures and personnel into place is only the first step towards data ethics management. An organization also needs to establish the processes by which these personnel will interact with the rest of the organization, and with each other, to achieve the business's data ethics goals. As the interviewees described them to us, these processes seemed to break down into two, somewhat overlapping, categories: processes for spotting data ethics issues and processes for reaching a decision about these issues. This chapter addresses each of these, in turn.

## 8.1 Processes for Spotting Data Ethics Issues

The interviewees described a number of issue spotting practices.

## 8.1.1 Touring the Business Units

Under the first, which we saw more in fast-paced, Silicon Valley companies, the team with primary responsibility for data ethics (e.g., data ethics office, or privacy office) largely assumed the issue spotting function. This team went out into the business units to meet with developers, learn about their projects, and help them to spot potential ethical issues. This model got the ethics team out of its office and into the business units, allowing it to problem-solve and address issues quickly. This may be why faster-paced, Silicon Valley-type companies preferred it. The disadvantage, however, is that it relies on a small group of individuals to spot ethical implications throughout the entire company and so can lead to important issues being missed. It does not scale. One ethics specialist explained just how challenging this can be:

> [O]ur team is small, there are 12 of us trying to support 2,000 deployments all over the world. I am currently at this year: 250,000 miles on [airline]. We are stretched very thin trying to keep up with everything . . . So in terms of flagging issues it is very spotty, and ad hoc and one of our big worries is something is going to happen that we're missing. And you think about code and how many million lines of code there is, how many complex, how many little decisions might actually have huge implications, it's difficult to figure out how to scale it in a way that would systematically catch everything." (Interviewee #10).

## 8.1.2 Hub and Spokes

The second approach was to place a junior privacy or ethics professional in each business unit. These professionals were trained to spot ethical issues and, where they such issues were significant and difficult to resolve, to refer them back to the central ethics team for further evaluation and resolution.[1] One interviewee referred to this as a "hub and spokes" model.

> [P]rivacy reviews are initially conducted by a privacy manager, which is typically a non-lawyer, sitting in a privacy team within the business. So we have sort of a hub and spoke model, where we have distributed a set of privacy managers who are out there in the business. Close to the business decision makers, close to the engineers, doing the privacy reviews according to the processes and standards that have been developed at the hub, in the center, and distributed it out. They are supposed to flag those issues. And the high-risk issues will get escalated to a legal person, who may then further escalate them to one of the central subject matter experts. . . . So there's a process for initial review, sort of issue spotting escalation. And that often works. . . . [H]aving that process in place is invaluable in that we do get eyes on these things very early, at different levels (Interviewee #16).

This decentralized, hub-and-spokes approach seemed to scale better than the centralized one. It appears to be gaining popularity, particularly among larger, more

---

[1] The "structure, from a management system's perspective, tends to be a privacy function with point people out into the business to make sure that there's good oversight and monitoring and that it ties back into an organizational-wide view." (Interviewee #22).

established companies that have many business units in which such ethical issues might arise.[2]

### 8.1.2.1 External Advisory Group

Some companies used an external advisory group to spot issues. Such a group—made up of privacy advocates, academics, industry people, former regulators, and others—gave the ethics officers a sense of what others might find troubling and so increased their sensitivity to potential ethical concerns. One referred to this as "pressure test[ing]" the company's future data practices from an external perspective.(Interviewee #9). Consulting with the external advisory group also gave the ethics team a way to gauge public expectations and so, consistent with the risk mitigation approach to data ethics, align the company's data practices with these expectations.

In some instances, the external advisory group provided the ethics team with additional leverage for advocating its views within the company. As one privacy and ethics leader put it, "we needed backup. We needed a credible group of people who could provide the really solid [feedback], who we could point to and say 'look, they agree with this analysis'.... So that's what it was initially formed as.... that's the sort of network we built up to do that... primarily academics, but we also wanted to get advocates in there." (Interviewee #10).

Some companies established sitting, external stakeholder committees. For example, one set up an external advisory board that included leading privacy advocates and academics. This board met regularly during the year and corresponded on a more ad hoc basis through emails. The interviewee explained that "they're under an NDA, [so] we can bounce ideas off them, we can show them deployments, we show them technologies, and get their feedback, so that catches things we might have missed, or gives us a perspective from outside the company which is very helpful." (Interviewee #10).

Other companies used a more ad hoc approach, convening groups of stakeholder experts to address particular issues when they arose. "We have the ability to contact consultants and people on the outside... and say, 'We're tackling with this issue, can you help us review this?' When do we do it?... [We do it] when we feel like the project is about something that we do not have in-house expertise in. And literally, if we feel like we're probably not the right people to review this, then we can go external." (Interviewee #14). This additional input can be helpful. For example, one interviewee

---

[2] An interviewee described this model as a "growing paradigm, and that is appointing people within each of the business units that are not only liaisons into a centralized privacy office or privacy function, but also they have responsibility for being the first point of review and oversight for whether or not that particular business unit is following the standards that have been established by the organization." Interviewee #22. In one company, the ethics team supplements its own capacity by partnering with the audit group which is already out in the business units. As the lead ethics officer explained, "I work very closely with internal audit. They'll be out doing what they normally do, and they'll see something and say, 'I heard this area's doing X,' and then we can go out, and take a look at it, and bring it into governance." Interviewee #16.

8.1 Processes for Spotting Data Ethics Issues

**Table 8.1** Does your company use an external advisory committee?

|  | Percent |
|---|---|
| No | 81.5 |
| Yes | 11.1 |
| I do not know | 7.4 |

recounted a time "when [a company that ran an Internet search engine] wanted to know if it was a good idea to give people the option of sharing all their searches on Facebook. And so they convened a consumer panel. They said it would be purely voluntary, but should we even allow it as an option? And the panel unanimously said no – you shouldn't allow people to trap themselves, because while they think there isn't any harm in that, you can come up with a parade of horribles from sharing your searches on Facebook." (Interviewee #23).

At the time of our research, the use of external data ethics advisory committees remained relatively uncommon. Even among the companies represented in the survey sample, only eleven percent utilized an external advisory committee for this purpose (Table 8.1). That said, the absence of a formal external committee did not necessarily mean companies were not seeking external insight informally.

Companies do need to be thoughtful about who they appoint to such external bodies. Google's appointment of a polarizing figure to such a group provoked such an adverse reaction that the company had to disband the group a week after creating it (Waters 2019).

### 8.1.2.2 Checklists

In his book The Checklist Manifesto: How to Get Things Right, Gawande (2009) popularized the idea that checklists can be a useful way for organizations to get their people to operationalize broad concepts and apply them consistently. Many industries and professions, including medicine, aviation and structural engineering, use them for this purpose. The interviewees indicated that some organizations are beginning to use data ethics checklists in order to get employees to operationalize and apply data ethics principles (Interviewee #19). One interviewee described their company's instrument as a "set of interrogatories that we're developing right now to get in front of the analytics teams that are going to be asking for data. It's based on some of [our data ethics] principles, but they're very simple questions, and they're more reflective. They get folks to think [about data ethics issues] before they take the deep dive into the data."(Interviewee #16).

The companies in our sample are still at an early stage in their development of data ethics checklists and were not able to make them available to us. A 2020 Microsoft Research article offers a resource for companies or policymakers interested in seeing what such a checklist might look like (Madaio et al. 2020). These researchers, which included a Carnegie Mellon Ph.D. candidate, conducted semi-structured interviews with fourteen data analytics practitioners to get a general sense of what these data scientists would look for in a data ethics checklist. They then engaged in an iterative process with 48 practitioners working on a variety of AI systems to co-design a model AI Fairness checklist.

The Microsoft Research team's interviews resonated in some ways with our interview findings. Practitioners explained to the Microsoft Research team that they found abstract data ethics principles to be hard to put into practice. They viewed checklists as a way to operationalize, and make more concrete, abstract concepts such as AI fairness. The practitioners also highlighted a potential downside to using checklists: they can breed a compliance-oriented mentality in which employees check the required boxes without engaging with the nuanced and context-based questions that data ethics issues often raise. In their view, checklists were best used to initiate reflection and conversation about issues such as fairness, bias, manipulation or transparency, rather than to provide discrete technical actions that engineers must follow. This fits with our finding, described above, that companies are coming to see data ethics as a strategic activity focused on improving the customer experience and building trust, and not as a compliance function.

The model AI Fairness checklist that the Microsoft Research team and practitioners co-designed, and that appears at the end of their article, consists of questions to consider, actions to take and items to document at six distinct stages in the product development process: (1) Envision (envisioning or greenlighting meetings); (2) Define (spec or design reviews); (3) Prototype (go/no-go discussions and code reviews); (4) Build (ship reviews); (5) Launch; and (6) Evolve (product reviews). Consisting of six sections, and running almost six pages, the checklist is quite long. But it becomes easier to comprehend when one realizes that it contains several core themes that are repeated throughout the various stages. These are:

- Identify those whom the AI system in question might impact, including particular demographic groups;
- Examine the types of fairness-related harms that the AI system might impose on such stakeholders (e.g., allocation, quality of service, stereotyping, denigration, over- or underrepresentation), how these compare to the system's benefits, and whether there are trade-offs between particular fairness criteria.
- Scrutinize and clarify definitions—of system architecture, datasets, potential fairness-related harms, fairness criteria and metrics—and revise them as necessary to mitigate any fairness-related harms.
- Solicit input from a diverse group of reviewers and stakeholders regarding vision, potential harms, definitions, fairness criteria, datasets, etc.
- Where feasible, test the product with these diverse reviewers so that they can better understand and provide feedback on them.
- Monitor product implementation for deviation from expectations and for anticipated or unanticipated fairness-related harms.
- Revise the vision, definitions, datasets, fairness criteria, prototype, etc. in order to mitigate potential harms.

- If it is not possible to mitigate the potential harm, explore and document why this is the case, future mitigation or contingency plans, and whether it makes sense to proceed with the project at all.
- Revise the system at regular intervals to improve its fairness performance and take account of changing social expectations or norms.

### 8.1.2.3 Sparking Discussion About Data Ethics Issues

Interviewees explained that regular reflection on and discussion of data ethics issues can help to build a culture in which people throughout the organization are more likely to spot and raise such issues. The idea is that developers and others need to become sensitized to these issues in order to be able to identify them, and that group discussion is an effective way to build this awareness.

Companies go about building this sensitivity and data ethics culture in various ways. One data ethics manager described their practice of circulating articles and other reports about data ethics incidents, concepts and solutions. "I'm really big on any article I get on data ethics, distributing it broadly,... These are what typically would be a garden variety way of communicating with people. But we're customizing it for data ethics. That's part of my ask from our leadership when they said, "How are we operationalizing this?" Communications is one of my performance goals, actually, so I'm working on it." (Interviewee #16).

The companies that we spoke with had not yet fully developed their techniques for initiating data ethics discussions in their organizations. However, the Omidyar Network has released a toolkit for sparking such data ethics discussions: the Ethical Explorer Pack.[3] This toolkit goes well beyond the ethical issues that business use of advanced analytics and AI can raise (the focus on this book) and considers a much wider range of data ethics risk areas. But organizations could adopt its approach for the ethical risks that their use of advanced analytics produces.

### 8.1.2.4 Peer-To-Peer Conversations

In a sign of just how important companies find ethical issue spotting to be, interviewees reported the emergence of informal, peer-to-peer, conversations to talk about ethical risks and how to address them. One interviewee who works in the Bay Area described off-the-record meetings of twenty or so privacy professionals to discuss the risks associated with advanced analytics and how best to deal with them. "The whole point is to really have a very genuine conversation about the topic, and a lot of people have started to convene them.... there's a lot of interest and activity around wanting to have these really genuine conversations." (Interviewee #2).

---

[3] https://ethicalexplorer.org/ (accessed 8 August 2023).

## 8.2 Processes for Deciding Data Ethics Issues

Once a company has spotted an ethical issue, the next step is to make a sound decision about it.

### 8.2.1 Just in Time Data Ethics

Where senior privacy or ethics executives go out into the business units to spot issues, they can often decide even difficult issues right away. This is the fastest approach. However, it quickly runs into resource constraints. "[T]he challenge is obviously that's not a process that scales very well. The bigger we get, the more difficult it is to have that in any consistent and meaningful way. So, it's an incredible challenge." (Interviewee #10).

#### 8.2.1.1 Triage and Escalation

The majority of companies that we spoke with employed the hub-and-spokes approach to issue spotting in which a junior person, located in the business unit, identifies issues and refers the hard ones back to the center. Such companies empowered the junior person to make decisions about relatively straightforward ethics issues that arose in their unit, perhaps after a quick consultation with the legal department. However, they required the person to escalate more complex, grey area issues to the more senior and seasoned decision-makers at the center.[4] One ethics lead analogized this triage and escalation approach to Institutional Review Boards that declare projects that raise few ethical issues to be "exempt" after only cursory review, and that reserve full IRB review for the more ethically complicated proposals (Interviewee #14). A leading consultant described it as "a basic risk assessment process that has escalateable decision points relative to the commensurate level of risk." (Interviewee #7). A third interviewee used a medical analogy:

> If you think about the concept of assessments, it's like a triaged process in an emergency room of the hospital. Somebody comes in, they have cuts and scrapes, I can deal with the

---

[4] One privacy and ethics leader explained that the "growing paradigm... is appointing people within each of the business units that are not only liaisons into a centralized privacy office or privacy function, but also they have responsibility for being the first point of review and oversight for whether or not that particular business unit is following the standards that have been established by the organization." The internal data ethics board resolves "higher-risk uses of data." (Interviewee #22). Another described a two-level process where "we have a number of specialists that evaluate it, send it around to a security person and a legal person and an engineer and we get agreement that it conforms to the rules and we sign off. It goes fast. Some of them are really, really big and we get in a room and it might take two weeks and we storyboard it out on a whiteboard. It takes a bunch of stakeholders. It's a heavy lift because it's something new and massive. Right? But we do about 800 a year. This is not something small. We do this at volume and scale." (Interviewee #6).

cuts and scrapes, I do not have to escalate to a doctor. I don't need to escalate that to the operating room. You have other people come in and they have broken bones that have to be set by a doctor, so you move to a second level of assessment to determine what is the right treatment level. You have a third level, a fourth level, then you have a level where the issues require assessment by a full range of people who have multiple skills, who will then decide whether what's being done is legal, fair and just (Interviewee #1).

### 8.2.1.2 The Role of the Data Ethics Committee

Once a complex ethical issue gets escalated, who decides it? Here, again, we see a distinction. Some companies, particularly Silicon Valley firms that emphasize speed and innovation, authorized a senior privacy or ethics official to make these calls. In at least one such company, this official was able to engage the CEO directly when necessary to reach a resolution (Interviewee #10). This yielded a quick, streamlined process in which the senior data ethics officer, backed by the CEO, were empowered to make decisions on behalf of the company.

Most of the companies we spoke with, however, established a cross-functional data ethics committee described in Chap. 7, rather than an individual, at the center of the decision-making process. Where privacy or ethics managers in the business units confronted difficult or novel issues that they could not comfortably resolve themselves, they referred it to such a committee.

> Many of the more sophisticated organizations... have started to set up these ethics review boards within the organization. So, it's not just about compliance. It's about thinking through these broader sets of data uses and thinking about whether or not they are meeting the company's standards for appropriate data use, if you will. Those tend to be more focused on areas of the business that are more likely to need them, so analytics groups... [or] research groups within organizations (Interviewee #22).

In one illustrative example, a data ethics committee considered whether the company should sell information technology to a customer who might, in turn, share it with the Chinese government for use in surveilling its population (Interviewee #2).[5]

The data ethics committee generally operated by consensus, with all members required to agree before an ethically challenging project can move forward (Interviewee #17). The group might tweak the project until all members were comfortable with it.[6] Some data ethics committees had the power to cancel projects or contracts where the committee believed that the risks are too high. Others were empowered only to make recommendations to the business units. In one important example of

---

[5] As noted above, this ethical question arose before the United States added these companies to the Entity List and so made such sales to them illegal.

[6] "I don't want this body... the cross functional review team... to start voting on things, because it just goes the wrong way, I think. So, I don't think that we've ever approved a project with a bigger team where people have not signed off. So, we essentially, will talk about it for as long as it takes for everybody to be okay with it. And it always happens." Where one member objects, the group "can massage it, we can massage it, we can massage it, and hopefully we'll reach a place where they can say, 'Yeah, okay. Now I'm okay with that.'" Interviewee #14.

the former approach, publicly reported in the media, Microsoft's AI and Ethics in Engineering and Research (AETHER) Committee vetoed major sales contracts on ethical grounds and put significant limits on others.[7]

Companies that wish to create a data ethics committee would do well to consider thoughtfully some important design choices. (Sandler and Basle 2019). These include:

- What types of expertise does this particular company need on its data ethics committee? Which perspectives are most important?
- Should the committee be able to consult with and get input from an external advisory group?
- Where should the committee be located within the organization? Privacy? Legal? Risk management? Strategy?
- To whom should it report? This person needs to be sufficiently high in the corporate hierarchy for the committee's judgements to carry weight.
- What standards should the committee use in making its decisions?
- Should the committee have the power to cancel projects or contracts, or only to make recommendations?
- Should the committee operate by consensus, or majority vote?
- How should issues be elevated to the committee? What process should be followed? What materials should be provided for committee consideration?
- How does the company define success for this committee? More ethical products? Fewer "incidents" that damage reputation?

## 8.3 Broader Themes

Several broader themes emerge from the interviewees' statements about management practices.

### 8.3.1 Streamlined Versus Deliberative

To begin with, one can see two basic corporate data ethics management approaches. The first is quick and streamlined. It sends decision-makers out into the business units where they spot issues and make just-in-time data ethics decisions. Where these executives do escalate thorny ethical problems back to the center, they come directly to a senior decision-maker who has a direct line to the C-Suite or CEO and is able to reach quick decisions about even the most complex issues.

---

[7] Geekwire, *Microsoft is Turning Down Some Sales Over AI Ethics, Top Researcher Eric Horvitz Says*, https://www.geekwire.com/2018/microsoft-cutting-off-sales-ai-ethics-top-researcher-eric-horvitz-says/ (accessed 8 August 2023).

The majority approach, however, is more deliberative and structured. It involves a hub-and-spokes approach to issue spotting; triage and escalation with respect to issue resolution; and a cross-functional data ethics committee to consider and reach decisions about the most difficult ethical issues, sometimes with input from an external advisory board. We loosely characterize these as "streamlined" and "deliberative" approaches to data ethics issue spotting and resolution.

Based on the interview data, we hypothesize that faster-paced, Silicon Valley-type companies tend to utilize the streamlined process. This gives them speed. However, it both increases the risk that the company may fail to spot certain ethical issues and arguably decreases the thoroughness, and so the quality, of the company's ethical decision-making. By contrast, more established companies appear to prioritize decision-making quality over speed. They insist that privacy or ethics officers in the field escalate difficult ethical decisions to the more senior executives at the center. They build a cross-functional data ethics committee to deliberate on and decide these complex issues. This takes longer. But it ensures that each decision is the product of a sustained, multi-perspective debate which can, in the most difficult cases, include referral to and input from an external advisory board. This should yield higher quality decisions.

Based on our rather limited interview sample, we further hypothesize that companies in the most highly regulated industries (e.g., heath care, pharmaceutical, financial, transportation, etc.) are more likely to have deliberative ethics decision-making systems, whereas those in newer, technology-oriented industries disproportionately adopt the streamlined approach. This may be because highly regulated companies are able to take legacy management structures developed for existing regulatory requirements and adapt them for the beyond compliance data ethics function.

Finally, we anticipate that the deliberate approaches will narrow the speed gap when compared to streamlined ones. They are likely to take the precedents that their cross-functional ethics committees produce and turn them into guidance for "spoke" decision-makers operating in the business units. This will, over time, enable the dispersed decision-makers to make more decisions, while referring fewer issues back to the committee itself. The speed differential between streamlined and deliberate decision-making processes should thus reduce over time, while the quality difference will remain. This should lead companies, even those in fast-paced industries, to prefer the more deliberate approach over the streamlined one.

### 8.3.2 Internal Versus System-Wide Focus

The interview data also suggests another important divide in corporate data ethics management processes. Some companies focused their data ethics efforts on their internal operations. Others looked not only at what the company itself is doing, but at the behavior of its suppliers and customers. They sought to achieve data ethics throughout the entire production system and value chain of which they are part.

Data ethics started with an internal focus. Soon after corporations began widely to use "big data" and advanced analytics, academics and privacy managers analogized this corporate activity to human subjects research in the university context. In an influential 2013 article, Professor Ryan Calo argued that companies should establish Consumer Subject Review Boards that would serve the same vetting function as Institutional Review Boards do in the university context (Calo 2013). This article helped to frame corporate data ethics management as a kind of private sector IRB focused on the company's own "human subjects" research.[8] One interviewee recounted that, as they started to build their company's data ethics process, "I really thought about the IRB model." (Interviewee #14).

Several interviewees expressed concerns about using the IRB model for data ethics. For one thing, IRBs in the university setting are notoriously slow. "It's not a fast and flexible system, and in the world of data driven applications, a month can be a killer for a project." (Interviewee #1). Second, an IRB faces internally. It focuses on and considers research projects that bubble up from the company itself. That is a vital function. But, according to some interviewees, it is not sufficient. In today's connected world, an organization's misbehavior profoundly impacts its business partner's. "You could have everybody doing the right thing, and you introduce one party into that process, whether it's the supplier of certain data or a processor that does a piece of the whole, and the weakness in that link is what's going to bring the whole thing down. The reputational impact... forget the compliance impact or the business continuity impact or investment impact." (Interviewee #21).

This same interviewee explained that, to account for important risks and protect its own reputation, a company's data ethics initiative must extend beyond its own ranks to include all entities in its value chain. It must seek to "ensure that each link in a chain or each part of the solution that's provided, that either contributes to or benefits from the predictive analytics, has to subject themselves to a certain competency and a certain set of diligence and a certain moral or ethical commitment to be part of that chain or ecosystem." (Interviewee #21). This suggests a distinction between those companies that focus their data ethics initiatives internally through an IRB model or otherwise; and those that take a system-wide approach that includes their suppliers, business partners and, in some cases, even customers.

Thus far, this narrative has focused on the management standards, structures and processes that organizations use to spot and decide difficult data ethics issues. But there is another side to data ethics management that focuses more on technical solutions to bias, opacity and other risks that innovative uses of data, advanced analytics and AI can generate. The next chapter conveys what we learned about technical solutions to data ethics challenges.

---

[8] For example, in 2013 the Future of Privacy Forum, a leading tech industry think tank, posted an interview with Professor Calo on the topic of Consumer Subject Review Boards, https://fpf.org/2013/08/28/podcast-talking-consumer-subject-review-boards-with-ryan-calo/ (accessed 8 August 2023). In 2015, it hosted a Roundtable titled *Beyond IRB's: Ethical Review Processes for Big Data Research*, https://fpf.org/2015/12/10/beyond-irbs-designing-ethical-review-processes-for-big-data-research/, (accessed 8 August 2023), that was attended by over 60 academics and industry researchers and at which Professor Calo gave a keynote address.

# References

Calo, Ryan. 2013. Consumer subject review boards: A thought experiment. *Stanford Law Review Online* 66: 97 (2013).

Gawande, Atul. 2009. *The Checklist Manifesto: How to Get Things Right*. New York: Metropolitan Books.

Madaio, Michael, Luke Stark, Jennifer Wortman Vaughan, and Hannah Wallach. 2020. *Co-Designing Checklists to Understand Organizational Challenges and Opportunities around Fairness in AI*.

Sandler, Ronald, and John Basle. 2019. *Building Data and AI Ethics Committees*. Northeastern University Ethics Institute & Accenture.

Waters, Richard. 2019. Google scraps ethics council for artificial intelligence. *Financial Times* (April 4, 2019).

**Open Access** This chapter is licensed under the terms of the Creative Commons Attribution 4.0 International License (http://creativecommons.org/licenses/by/4.0/), which permits use, sharing, adaptation, distribution and reproduction in any medium or format, as long as you give appropriate credit to the original author(s) and the source, provide a link to the Creative Commons license and indicate if changes were made.

The images or other third party material in this chapter are included in the chapter's Creative Commons license, unless indicated otherwise in a credit line to the material. If material is not included in the chapter's Creative Commons license and your intended use is not permitted by statutory regulation or exceeds the permitted use, you will need to obtain permission directly from the copyright holder.

# Chapter 9
# Technical Solutions

**Abstract** This chapter reviews the technological solutions that organizations leverage to ensure the ethical management and downstream use of collected data for building analytic and AI models. Survey respondents discussed solutions that ranged from privacy preserving data management strategies such as differential privacy, to the use of virtualization and data lake control systems for secure access. Survey respondents also keyed in on the clear and pressing need for data and algorithmic auditing technology and systems to support ethical data governance. With respect to how such data is used ethically, respondents identified the importance of algorithmic fairness as well as model transparency as essential to help identify and also mitigate risks associated with real world modeling failures.

**Keywords** Differential privacy · Fair models · Explainable AI · Algorithmic auditing · Data security · Access controls

---

**Key Take-Aways**

- **Technical methods**. This chapter discusses the technical methods that companies deployed at the time we conducted our research (2017–2019) to make their use of advanced analytics and AI fairer, more privacy protective, and more explainable.
- **Techniques for privacy-protective data analysis**. To improve privacy performance, the companies considered technology-based approaches such as k-anonymity, l-diversity, and epsilon-differential privacy. At the time of our study, differential privacy was the de facto standard for privacy preserving data analysis.
- **Techniques for achieving fairer AI and ML**. Companies emphasized the importance of technological solutions to facilitate fairer artificial intelligence and machine learning (ML). At the time of our research, organizations were only beginning to utilize data statements, fact sheets, and model

---

© The Author(s) 2024
D. Hirsch et al., *Business Data Ethics*,
SpringerBriefs in Law,
https://doi.org/10.1007/978-3-031-21491-2_9

cards. They are being used more broadly today and we expect this trend to continue.
- **Techniques for making advanced analytics and AI more explainable.** Contemporary models that employ billions of parameters to inform decisions about people have made algorithmic explainability critical, at the same time as they make it harder to achieve. Some interviewees maintained that, even more important than explaining the models themselves, it was critical to explain why models fail and the risks associated with such failure.
- **Techniques for auditing.** To achieve its ethical goals, an organization must be able to audit its algorithms and measure whether, in fact, they align with these goals. At the time of our research, organizations were beginning to increase their work on algorithmic auditing tools and the use of data provenance in the development of such auditing solutions.
- **Systems technologies.** Several companies discussed their use of systems technologies to enable or enhance their governance advanced analytics and AI. These included the use of controlled data warehouses or data lakes to ensure credentialed access. Others employed virtualization as a way to represent all of an organization's data in one place and so improve access controls.

Trust is an important lubricant of the modern economy. It is not only a nice thing to have and foster; it has, as the economist Arrow said back in the 1970s, a very important pragmatic value. As noted previously in this book, trust serves as a central motivation for corporate data ethics generally and, more specifically, for why corporations and organizations are increasingly turning to technological solutions to data ethics issues. In this chapter we focus on some of these technological solutions, specifically on data privacy, fairness in AI algorithms, and analytic and management tools that several of our interviewees touch upon as they relate to ethical governance through technology. Most of our research subjects were data privacy and ethics professionals whose expertise lies in the management and process-based solutions discussed in earlier chapters of this book. But the interviewees made clear that technological solutions, too, were crucial to data ethics management and spoke at some length about them. This chapter conveys what we learned about the technical dimension of data ethics management as practiced at the time of the interviews (2017–2019).

## 9.1 Data Privacy and Anonymization

Almost all of our interviewees brought up the importance of data privacy and anonymization. Modern technology-based efforts to protect privacy include research efforts on k-anonymity, (Sweeney 2002), l-diversity (Machanavajjhala et al. 2007) and epsilon-differential privacy (or differential privacy for short) (Dwork et al. 2014).

## 9.1 Data Privacy and Anonymization

The interviews made clear that, at the time of our interviews, differential privacy was the current de facto standard for privacy preserving data analysis. (Dwork 2019). As one interviewee stated:

> We have a policy called differential privacy which is heavily utilized by a lot of the largest tech companies but way less utilized by the rest of the world. We basically automated our own implementation of it. What differential privacy does is it provides mathematical guarantees that you could never actually get down to the value of a specific cell based on the answer you're getting from any query. So, it's a mathematical way to try to guarantee privacy. (Interviewee #5).

Several interviewees also discussed simpler, rule-based aggregation strategies for anonymization and de-identification aligned with the classical notions of k-anonymity. For example, one, explaining that their company only provides aggregate information to others, stated that the company had rules in place to protect individual privacy. For instance, "[I]f there were only fewer than five people that had a particular issue then we wouldn't share even the analysis, or the outcome, or the summary of that, because we thought it would be too close to identifying a particular set of users." (Interviewee #4). Another interviewee summarized a number of privacy-protective strategies:

> [T]hose vary from masking, which hides the values of particular cells in a table, in different ways. It can be hashing, it can be generalization, it can be replacing with one specific value. So, for example, replace the last four digits of every social security number . . . with four zeros. . . . We can restrict what . . . data is usable based on time. We could create a rule that says only show the last six months of data. We have what's called minimization polices where you could say, "Only allow users to access statistically representative example of X percentage of this data set." You can create that policy and you can set that percentage to whatever you want. (Interviewee #5).

Implicit in much of this discussion is the tradeoff between privacy and utility to both the end user and the organization managing the data. While differential privacy was at the time of the interviews, and remains today, the de-facto standard, active research is underway on how to improve existing solutions against new types of attacks (Cheu et al. 2021; Zhao and Chen 2022), the deployment of homomorphic encryption that allows for training on encrypted data directly (Phong et al. 2018; Abadi et al. 2016), and the use of federated learning to distribute training to edge devices thereby enhancing privacy while also giving users greater control over how their data is used in model training (Li et al. 2020).

The interviewees noted that privacy, as protected by these technical solutions, overlaps with, but is not synonymous with, ethics. Organizations that protect privacy can still utilize data in ways that are ethically problematic. As one interviewee put it:

> I think data ethics is much larger than privacy. It's not just about whether I keep somebody's data private. I can aggregate people's data in ways where they remain private, but they become part of a cohort where predictive analytics uses their data, with respect to that group, in ways

that an ethicist might say are not appropriate, or does projects, that while using anonymous data ... [is] a project that an ethicist might say, "You shouldn't be doing." (Interviewee #5).[1]

In short, while tools that support privacy and anonymization—including ideas like privacy by design (Cavoukian 2012)—are essential to an ethical business data framework, they are not sufficient in themselves to ensure ethical application of advanced analytics.

## 9.2 Algorithmic Fairness

Several interviewees brought up the importance of algorithmic fairness, fair data use, and its connection to data ethics governance (Kleinberg et al. 2018; Wilkinson et al. 2016). They point out a clear need for technological solutions to facilitate fair artificial intelligence (AI) and Machine Learning (ML). For example, some companies make an effort to find and use datasets that are both inclusive of marginalized groups (so that the resulting AI does not treat them less accurately) and, at the same time, are not themselves shaped by harmful societal bias. Laws are beginning to require this. For example, New York City's Fair Chance Act makes it illegal for most employers in the city to ask about the criminal record of an applicant seeking a job. One data ethics manager explained how her company tried to address such issues as follows:

> These could be questions like does this dataset impact communities of color or- does this data set include information about people who are already disproportionately disadvantaged, that sort of thing. If the data set had the potential to ... cause more or less bias, there was an escalation path... A set of specific labels. You know, low, medium and high that has different escalation path as to how or when that data set will be approved for purchase, work, or use. (Interviewee #2).

Some interviewees also pointed out the need to have fair and private algorithms that minimize risk and yet have utility, pointing to the inherent pareto-optimality often involved. One interviewee explained that "with *the Ebola epidemic, there could have been more accurate predictive models of the spread, if the cell phone companies had been willing to share data, but they were so afraid to do so . . . [They were afraid because of] [p]rivacy. An epidemiologist was arguing that, 'No, you can't do that because there's a risk of re-identification.'"* (Interviewee #3). At the time of the interviews, algorithmic fairness was still relatively nascent and had not been widely adopted. We expect that tools that facilitate the creation of data statements (Bender and Friedman 2018), fact sheets (Arnold et al. 2019), and model cards (Mitchell et al. 2019), are likely to find their way to being used more broadly in the near term.

---

[1] Another interviewee made a similar point: "*I can still misuse data using differential privacy - it doesn't ask me what my query is, it's going to keep me from identifying anybody, but if I use the tool to identify who is gay based on certain data points, differential privacy isn't going to say to me: 'Hey, that's not a good [ethical] research element,'' even though it would prevent me from identifying any individual.*'" (Interviewee #19).

## 9.3 The Clear and Pressing Need for Explainable Algorithms

Somewhat related to, and yet distinct from, the notion of fair algorithms is the ability to understand what these complex ML and AI algorithms are exactly doing under the hood. (Samek et al. 2019; Gunning and Aha 2019). Explainability and model transparency facilitates trust and ensures regulatory policies are being met.

Explainability in data analysis and AI is not a new topic. A famous early example was during the 1854 outbreak of Cholera in London where Dr. John Snow presented authorities with a simple cluster map showing that the disease spread clustered around a water pump on Broad Street in London convincing them to take action (Tulchinsky 2018). Explainability in AI dates back at least four decades to expert systems that explained their results via decision rule (Mitchell et al. 1986). The current emphasis on explainability arises largely from the fact that contemporary models are much more complex (some with several billion parameters) and are increasingly used to make critical decisions. Justifying such decisions in the presence of increasing regulatory requirements amplifies the need for explainability in such models (Biran and Cotton 2017).

Several of the interviewees emphasized the importance of explainability. One explained that explainability is key to ethical data governance. One pointed out that explainability is critical to trust. (Interviewee #9). Another described how difficult it can be to explain models and how the company arrived at them:

> When we get into AI and machine learning, sometimes it's pretty challenging to describe, to understand what transparency means. In the old days you could say, we take an email address, and we look at your purchase history. And we decide what products you might be interested in buying based on your past purchase history, and we will send you targeted marketing based on that. That was pretty straightforward. People can understand that, but when you have thousands of data inputs developing and machines discovering correlations that might not be intuitively obvious, [and companies] building profiles and customizing a variety of experiences based on that, not only is it harder to explain, in some cases it might be impossible to explain to that same level, because there is no human who understands what correlations are being drawn. (Interviewee #12).

While explainability of analytic and AI models is highly important, it can also be challenging. First, as was already noted, the increasing scale and complexity of modern models makes them harder to understand and to explain. Second, explainability requirements vary depending on whether the target user is an end-user, a domain expert (e.g., clinician) or a data scientist. Third, context matters. Explainability requirements depend on the task, abilities of the human-in-the-loop, socio-cultural expectations and the regulatory requirements of the environment. Finally, some interviewees pointed out that one may have to go beyond simple explainability and consider explanations as to why models fail and the need to understand risks associated with such failure. As one interviewee stated:

> Usually the first thing they spend most of their time focusing on is explainability . . . A lot of that is, quite frankly, true, but focusing only on explainability, I think, obscures the

larger picture. Our point . . . is risk management and failure mitigation . . . . From a risk management perspective, there are a variety of different ways and processes and things we can do to help govern these models even if we don't explain them . . . . Think about failure. What does failure mean to you? As a company how would you react? What processes are in place? . . . . One of the downsides of models that are hard to explain is when they fail, it's hard to understand why. (Interviewee #5).

## 9.4 Algorithmic Auditing of Data Use

The modern economy is increasingly reliant on our ability to generate and store large tracts of data and realize actionable insights from this data. The algorithmic steps by which these insights are discerned and subsequently shared are often complex—requiring multiple transformative steps. These complex multi-step processes in turn can lead to several sources of risk at each step. The ability to mitigate such risk requires the ability to audit the algorithms to ensure that stated ethical data governance policies and regulatory requirements are being met (Raji et al. 2020). At the time of the interviews, organizations were beginning to examine how best to audit whether algorithms meet predetermined specifications.

> Next year, we're actually going to begin auditing. Part of making sure we're doing what we need to do is to make sure another set of eyes comes in, and we're going to be opening up to audit the request, the conditions, the compliance with those requests, and the assurance the data is being used the way we directed them to use it. (Interviewee #16).

While such efforts date back to the Gedanken-experiments on black box automaton machines by E. F. Moore in 1950s (Moore 1956), research has largely been sporadic until the recent, widespread use of AI-based decision-making increased the importance of algorithmic auditing tools (Cooper et al. 2022; Maneriker et al. 2023) and the use of data provenance (Buneman et al. 2001) in the development of such auditing solutions. One interviewee explained that:

> We characterize all the data sources, understand the data provenance, how we're bringing the data together, how we're transforming it, how we're activating it, what it's going to used for, what the controls are . . . we go through and we measure for things like hidden bias or hidden discrimination. We measure for accuracy [of algorithms] and accuracy occurs on a continuum. If you're delivering a fraud product, you need to be very accurate. If it's a marketing product, the accuracy is not quite as imperative as it is when you're doing identity authentication. (Interviewee #6).

## 9.5 Systems Technologies to Enable Governance

Several interviewees talked about technical systems that they use to enable or enhance governance of data science. Some employ controlled data warehouses or data lakes (a federated set of datasets including both structured and unstructured data in raw form) (Jarke et al. 1999; Ramakrishnan et al. 2017), as a means of ensuring credentialed access only by trusted individuals within an organization.

> When we talk to the data lake team or the data governance team, this is a point that we make absolutely clear to them, that at no point would this data transfer or be pulled from the data lake environment or from a secondary source from data lake and back into any of the credit systems.... There are administrative and physical controls... different users are basically confined to play in their space. (Interviewee #17).

Another talked about the use of "virtualization... virtually representing data without actually using it or copying it" as a way to "represent all data across an organization in one single place" and so provide an effective access control mechanism. (Interviewee #5) (Singh et al. 2008; Soror et al. 2007). Virtualization can also assist in addressing the "reproducibility crisis" in machine learning[2]—the situation in which data scientists often cannot reproduce results across teams. (Interviewee #5). One interviewee explained that increased formalization of machine learning, through virtualization and other means, is essential to establishing governance of it. The question is how to do this without constraining data scientists and stifling creativity and innovation.

> [T]here's a crisis in the world of data science and data scientists are basically incapable of reproducing their results across teams. And that's a product of many things. But largely it's just a product of how informal the worlds they live in are. And so, if one data scientist leaves the team and leaves the organization and another data scientist comes in, frequently they have to start from scratch. And it's a crisis as you start to rely on the models they're developing more and more. But it is squarely a governance topic in my thinking . . . because if data scientists can't confidently reproduce what's going on, how can lawyers and governance and people thinking about risk, how can all of these personnel justify these decisions and justify the risks embedded in them? So, I think there has to be, for a variety of reasons, a move towards formalization and the trick is just going to be can organizations do it without over-correcting and can they do it without stifling creativity. (Interviewee #5).

In sum, we find that technological support for privacy and anonymization is necessary and essential but not sufficient. Both algorithmic fairness and explainability of AI and ML algorithms are important to ensure ethical governance. The ability to understand the provenance of data transformations as well as the ability to audit algorithms that process such data is also essential as are systems technologies that provide for access control and data virtualization and management.

# References

Abadi, Martin, Andy Chu, Ian Goodfellow, H. Brendan McMahan, Ilya Mironov, Kunal Talwar, and Li Zhang. 2016. Deep learning with differential privacy. In *Proceedings of the 2016 ACM SIGSAC Conference on Computer and Communications Security*, 308–318. New York: ACM.

Arnold, Matthew, Rachel KE Bellamy, Michael Hind, Stephanie Houde, Sameep Mehta, A Mojsilović, Ravi Nair, K. Natesan Ramamurthy, Alexandra Olteanu, David Piorkowski, Jason Tsay, and Kush R. Varshney. FactSheets: Increasing trust in AI services through supplier's declarations of conformity. *IBM Journal of Research and Development* 63 (4/5): 6:1–6:13.

---

[2] https://petewarden.com/2018/03/19/the-machine-learning-reproducibility-crisis/ (accessed 8 August 2023).

Bender, Emily M., Batya Friedman. 2018. Data statements for natural language processing: Toward mitigating system bias and enabling better science. *Transactions of the Association for Computational Linguistics* 6: 587–604.
Biran, Or, and Courtenay Cotton. Explanation and justification in machine learning: A survey. *IJCAI-17 Workshop on Explainable AI (XAI)* 8 (1): 1–6.
Buneman, Peter, Sanjeev Khanna, and Wang Chiew Tan. 2001. Why and where: A characterization of data provenance. *ICDT* 2001: 316–330.
Cavoukian, Ann. 2012. Privacy by design. *IEEE Technology and Society Magazine* 31 (4): 18–19.
Cheu, Albert, Adam Smith, and Jonathan Ullman. 2021. Manipulation attacks in local differential privacy. In *IEEE Symposium on Security and Privacy*, 883–900. San Francisco, CA.
Cooper, A.F., E. Moss, B. Laufer, and H. Nissenbaum. 2022. Accountability in an algorithmic society: Relationality, responsibility, and robustness in machine learning. In *Proceedings of the 2022 ACM Conference on Fairness, Accountability, and Transparency*, 864–876.
Dwork, Cynthia, and Aaron Roth. 2014. The algorithmic foundations of differential privacy. *Foundations and Trends in Theoretical Computer Science* 9 (3–4): 211–407.
Dwork, Cynthia. 2019. Differential privacy and the US census. In *Proceedings of the 38th ACM SIGMOD-SIGACT-SIGAI Symposium on Principles of Database Systems*. New York, NY: ACM.
Gunning, David, and David W. Aha. 2019. DARPA's explainable artificial intelligence. *(XAI) Program AI Magazine* 40 (2): 44–58.
Jarke, M., M. Lenzerini, and Y. Vassiliou, eds. 1999. *Fundamentals of Data Warehousing*, 1999. Berlin-Heidelberg, Germany: Springer-Verlag.
Kleinberg, Jon, Jens Ludwig, Sendhil Mullainathan, and Ashesh Rambachan. 2018. Algorithmic fairness. *AEA Papers and Proceedings* 108: 22–27.
Li, Tian, Anit Kumar Sahu, Ameet Talwalkar, and Virginia Smith. 2020. Federated learning: Challenges, methods, and future directions. *IEEE Signal Processing Magazine* 37 (3): 50–60.
Machanavajjhala, Ashwin, Daniel Kifer, Johannes Gehrke, and Muthuramakrishnan Venkitasubramaniam. 2007. L-diversity: Privacy beyond k-anonymity. *ACM Transactions on Knowledge Discovery from Data* 1 (1): 3.
Maneriker, P., C. Burley, and S. Parthasarathy. 2023. Online fairness auditing through iterative refinement. In *Proceedings of the 2023 ACM Conference on Knowledge Discovery and Data Mining*, 1665–1676. New York: ACM.
Mitchell, Margaret, Simone Wu, Andrew Zaldivar, Parker Barnes, Lucy Vasserman, Ben Hutchinson, Elena Spitzer, Inioluwa Deborah Raji, and Timnit Gebru. 2019. Model cards for model reporting. In *Proceedings of the Conference on Fairness, Accountability, and Transparency*, 220–229. New York: ACM.
Mitchell, Tom M., Richard M. Keller, and Smadar T. Kedar-Cabelli. 1986. Explanation-based generalization: A unifying view. *Machine Learning* 1 (1): 47–80.
Moore, Edward F. 1956. Gedanken-experiments on sequential machines. *Automata Studies* 34: 129–153.
Phong, Le Trieu, Yoshinori Aono, Takuya Hayashi, Lihua Wang, and Shibo Moriai. Privacy-Preserving Deep Learning Via Additively Homomorphic Encryption. *IEEE Transactions on Information Forensics and Security* 13 (5): 1333–1345.
Raji, Inioluwa Deborah, Andrew Smart, Rebecca N. White, Margaret Mitchell, Timnit Gebru, Ben Hutchinson, Jamila Smith-Loud, Daniel Theron, and Parker Barnes. 2020. Closing the AI accountability gap: defining an end-to-end framework for internal algorithmic auditing. In *Proceedings of the 2020 Conference on Fairness, Accountability, and Transparency*, 33–44. New York: ACM.
Ramakrishnan, Raghu, Baskar Sridharan, John R. Douceur, Pavan Kasturi, Balaji Krishnamachari-Sampath, Karthick Krishnamoorthy, Peng Li, Mitica Manu, Spiro Michaylov, Rogério Ramos, Neil Sharman, Zee Xu, Youssef Barakat, Chris Douglas, Richard Draves, Shrikant S. Naidu, Shankar Shastry, Atul Sikaria, Simon Sun, and Ramarathnam Venkatesan. 2017. Azure data lake store: A hyperscale distributed file service for big data analytics. In *SIGMOD Conference 2017*, 51–63.

# References

Samek, Wojciech, Grégoire Montavon, Andrea Vedaldi, Lars Kai Hansen, Klaus-Robert Müller. 2019. Explainable AI: Interpreting, explaining and visualizing deep learning. Lecture Notes in Computer Science 11700, Springer 2019, ISBN 978-3-030-28953-9.

Singh, Aameek, Madhukar R. Korupolu, and Dushmanta Mohapatra. 2008. Server-storage virtualization: Integration and load balancing in data centers. *SC 2008*: 53.

Soror, A.A., A. Aboulnaga, and K. Salem. 2007. Database virtualization: A new frontier for database tuning and physical design. In 2007 *IEEE 23rd International Conference on Data Engineering Workshop*, 388–394, Istanbul.

Sweeney, Latanya. 2002. k-Anonymity: A model for protecting privacy. *International Journal of Uncertainty Fuzziness Knowledge Based Systems* 10 (5): 557–570.

Tulchinsky, Theordore H. 2018. John snow, cholera, the broad street pump; waterborne diseases then and now. *Case Studies in Public Health* 2018: 77–99.

Wilkinson, M., M. Dumontier, I. Aalbersberg, et al. 2016. The FAIR guiding principles for scientific data management and stewardship. *Science Data* 3: 160018.

Zhao, Ying, and Jinjun Chen. 2022. A survey on differential privacy for unstructured data content. *ACM Computing Surveys* 54 (10): 207:1–207:28.

**Open Access** This chapter is licensed under the terms of the Creative Commons Attribution 4.0 International License (http://creativecommons.org/licenses/by/4.0/), which permits use, sharing, adaptation, distribution and reproduction in any medium or format, as long as you give appropriate credit to the original author(s) and the source, provide a link to the Creative Commons license and indicate if changes were made.

The images or other third party material in this chapter are included in the chapter's Creative Commons license, unless indicated otherwise in a credit line to the material. If material is not included in the chapter's Creative Commons license and your intended use is not permitted by statutory regulation or exceeds the permitted use, you will need to obtain permission directly from the copyright holder.

# Chapter 10
# Data Analytics for the Social Good

**Abstract** This chapter describes instances in which companies intentionally use advanced analytics and AI to serve the social good without any direct benefit to their own bottom lines. Broadly speaking, we found two types of "social good" projects. Some employed approaches to learn about, and inform individuals of, risks or opportunities to improve their lives. Others provided information to public bodies that enabled them to improve their planning efforts or efficiency, such as utilizing location data to improve evacuation planning during natural disasters or to track infectious diseases. The research suggested that companies are cognizant of the need to attend both to moral values and to the interests of a broad set of stakeholders, and of the fact that doing so can build trust and contribute to the company's own well-being. In our study, many companies expressed a willingness to enter into beyond compliance ethical thinking in recognition of the convergence of their own business interests with the demands of trustworthy and responsible decision-making. These efforts raise interesting questions about companies' moral obligation to pursue the public good and how companies will behave when the public and corporate good diverge.

**Keywords** AI for good · Beneficial AI · Social good · Business ethics

> **Key Take-Aways**
>
> - **Some companies use AI for the social good.** "AI for the social good" projects benefit others without directly improving the company's bottom line. Some companies undertake such projects.
> - **The "social good" projects in our study were of two types.** Some employed advanced analytics to learn about, and inform individuals of, risks they faced or ways they could improve their lives. Others provided information to public bodies that enabled them to improve their planning efforts or efficiency.

- **Blended motivations.** The research suggested that companies are cognizant both of the need to attend to moral values and to the interests of a broad set of stakeholders, and of the fact that doing so can build trust and contribute to the company's own well-being.
- **What are the limits?** These efforts raise interesting questions about companies' moral obligation to pursue the public good, the limits of this obligation, and how companies will behave when the public and corporate good diverge. Privately-held corporations with socially conscious employees and/or CEO's appear more likely to pursue the social good even when doing so might work, to some extent, against the company's interest.

As companies grapple with the need to go "beyond compliance" in their data ethics practices, some of them have embraced opportunities to use advanced analytics for the social good. These efforts are distinguished from other advanced analytics and AI projects in that they seek to advance the public interest without directly benefiting the company's own bottom line (although they may generate longer-term reputational benefits). Several interviewees described projects of this type. As one study participant put it: "there's something intuitive in the idea that this is still everybody's data and that it should somehow and someway benefit everybody." (Interviewee #20). Efforts to promote the social good exemplify the oft-repeated refrain among our interviewees that, in going beyond compliance, their companies are trying to do "the right thing" and not merely embracing morally good options because they enhance customer or public trust, or otherwise advance their business interests.

These "data analytics for the social good" efforts seem to fall into two main baskets. First, advanced analytics and AI may allow companies to warn individuals of risks or to help them discover opportunities to improve their lives. A well-known and controversial example of this sort is Facebook's suicide prevention program. Facebook used advanced analytics and AI to identify, based on a user's activity, whether that person was potentially suicidal. In March 2017, the company began scanning users' activity for pre-suicidal signals, and then sharing with the user information about how to obtain support, or, in some cases, notifying emergency responders.[1] In the second category of "social good" projects, companies produce socially valuable information for municipalities or other public bodies to improve their planning or efficiency. Our interviews reveal a number of such examples, such as utilizing location data to improve evacuation planning during natural disasters, track infectious diseases, or relieve traffic congestion in cities.

Companies' involvement in these "social good" efforts raise a series of important questions. To what extent are these efforts motivated by the companies' long-term interest in gaining the trust of customers or the public? Will companies continue the efforts at such time as promoting the social good no longer benefits the company? How do such initiatives get started within companies, and how can they be sustained?

---

[1] https://www.businessinsider.com/facebook-is-using-ai-to-try-to-predict-if-youre-suicidal-2018-12 (accessed 8 August 2023).

Finally, are companies morally obligated to try to "do the right thing" over and above respecting certain legal constraints as they pursue their business interests? These questions have long been at the heart of debates about corporate social responsibility.[2]

The Business Roundtable made headlines in August 2019 when it stated that companies should not focus primarily on shareholder value, but instead should embrace a broader commitment to all stakeholders. Alex Gorsky, Chairman of the Board and Chief Executive Officer of Johnson and Johnson, said about the statement: "It affirms the essential role corporations can play in improving our society when CEOs are truly committed to meeting the needs of all stakeholders" (Business Roundtable 2019). At a minimum, this suggests that moral values and regard for the interests of a broad set of affected individuals (and not just shareholder or executive self-interest bounded only by legal compliance) should inform corporate decision-making in an integrated way. But what are the limits of this commitment, in principle and in practice?[3]

Consider the competing motivations driving many corporate social responsibility (CSR) programs. Philanthropy and other ways of connecting with the community that go beyond core business services or products may be motivated by a desire to promote the social good. But they are often also motivated by a company's own interest in enhancing its reputation. What might it mean for a company to pursue CSR in the spirit of the Business Roundtable statement? Rangan et al. have argued that although an effective and appropriate CSR program must reflect a company's overall "business purpose and values," it should avoid being consciously directed by narrow business aims. Improved business outcomes "should be spillover, not their reason for being:"

> Some [CSR] initiatives indeed create shared value; some, though intended to do so, create more value for society than for the firm; and some are intended to create value primarily for society. Yet all have one thing in common: They are aligned with the companies' business purpose, the values of the companies' important stakeholders, and the needs of the communities in which the companies operate. These companies, of course, stand in stark contrast to those that are focused solely on creating value for their shareholders. (Rangan, et al. 2015)

Our study reinforces the thought that, for many practitioners, "doing the right thing" is typically meant in this spirit. Companies are cognizant of the need to attend to moral values and to the interests of a broad set of stakeholders, and they may welcome opportunities to pursue the social good independent of any immediate business aim. But the pursuit of the social good cannot be entirely divorced from the company's business purpose. Doing "the right thing," then, typically refers to the company's conscious willingness to go beyond legal compliance into less certain moral territory, to try to live up to what a responsible company is expected to do, and to welcome opportunities where its business purpose and values coincide with

---

[2] The literature on corporate social responsibility is vast (Carroll 1999, 2008; Mulligan 1993; Preston 1975; Sheehy 2015; Vogel 2005).

[3] Decisions by major corporations during the COVID epidemic to cut their workforces while continuing to pay out hundreds of millions in dividends to shareholders suggests the Business Roundtable statement has not had much effect.

the social good. But the key practical question that practitioners must address is not "what's the right thing to do" in some idealized sense, but rather "how can a company be a responsible member of society," especially in uncertain terrain.

This idea of the motivation for, and limits of, pursuing the social good for its own sake is reflected in the ambiguities in many study participants' comments on such efforts. Take these examples from two interviewees and a recent report:

> To achieve loyalty and trust from users while constantly evolving and offering new products and services, companies must do more than implement good data practices—they must build a culture of privacy and security that embeds and formalizes values of digital dignity and data stewardship and contributes to the social good. (de Mooy and Yuen 2016)
>
> Yes, we definitely have [talked publicly about social good projects]. It ranges from … press releases that we have done where we've talked about it or in conjunction with a university or a city or things of that nature. When I speak externally, I always talk about it if the forum presents itself because I think it shows how you can build a program and try to enhance your reputation as a company that cares for data and you develop that trust factor or that transparency factor with the external environment, whether it's your customers or regulators or the press or the media or whoever is part of the audience. (Interviewee #9)
>
> I do see us as a single corporate culture about putting our customers first and doing the right thing. And giving back to the community and being trustworthy. (Interviewee #20)

These passages highlight the key question of motivation and the limiting case where a company's interest and the social good diverge.

Our study offers some clues about how companies may remain committed to the social good even at some cost to business interests. A lot depends on individuals within the company themselves remaining committed to the projects and offering their time, effort, and leadership. Sometimes this can work in a bottom-up fashion: "I would say it usually starts with individual teams, individual people. And then, they escalate it and say, 'We think that we should do this'... And then, obviously, that goes up the chain... It started from the bottom up." (Interviewee #14). This in turn suggests that companies that want to remain committed to the social good have reason to bring in employees who will be sensitive to moral issues or other stakeholder concerns. "[H]ire individuals with a background or experience in... sociology, ethics, and/or human subject research.... Distributing this talent throughout the organization will embed a value of data stewardship throughout the decision-making and review processes" (de Mooy and Yuen 2016, at 17).

But more commonly companies that pursue the social good are able to maintain that stance because of the commitment of their CEO, which in turn informs the corporate culture. Study participants often invoked the influence of leadership on the way the whole company functions.

> I've heard our CEO bemoan the fact that some of the really large data companies internationally have done virtually nothing to help with their data, and [the CEO] believes that's profoundly wrong. (Interviewee #20)
>
> I don't know why some companies care about things they're not legally required to care about.... As I looked inside of [company], at the time, there was a philosophy in the company around responsibility and doing the right thing. It changed, but it was there. And kind of part of DNA of the company. . . . We had an incredibly strong CEO at the time that cared about responsible practices and going above and beyond. We had an even stronger general

counsel... I almost think that it comes down to just this perfect storm of the company's history and philosophy around social responsibility. (Interviewee #2)

It perhaps goes without saying that privately held companies have even more flexibility to reflect the values of the owner or other leadership.

In summary, then, companies have long recognized claims of corporate social responsibility that require going beyond compliance. As companies enter the world of data ethics, they will encounter many opportunities to benefit their communities through advanced analytics and AI. Some companies are already looking for these opportunities and they recognize that, in competitive fields where customer and public trust is vital, pursuing the social good often coincides with their long-term interests. Whether most companies will integrate moral values and the broader interests of the public into their decision-making *for their own sake*, and not because of the coincidence of morality and interest, remains an open question.

# References

Business Roundtable. 2019. Business Roundtable Redefines the Purpose of a Corporation to Promote 'An Economy That Serves All Americans.' Available at https://www.businessroundtable.org/business-roundtable-redefines-the-purpose-of-a-corporation-to-promote-an-economy-that-serves-all-americans. Accessed August 8, 2023.

Carroll, Archie B. 1999. Corporate social responsibility: evolution of a definitional construct. *Business & Society* 38(3): 268–295.

Carroll, Archie B. 2008. A history of corporate social responsibility: concepts and practices. In *The oxford handbook of corporate social responsibility*, eds. Crane Andrew, Dirk Matten, Abagail McWilliams, Jeremy Moon and Donald S. Siegel, 19–46. New York: Oxford University Press.

de Mooy, Michelle, and Shelten Yuen. 2016. *In Wearable Health: Towards Privacy-Aware Research and Development* 20.

Mulligan, Thomas M. 1993. The moral mission of business. In *Ethical theory and business*, eds. Tom L. Beauchamp and Norman E. Bowie (4th ed.), 65–75. Englewood Cliffs, NJ: Prentice Hall.

Preston, Lee E, and James E. Post. 1975. *Private management and public policy: the principle of public responsibility*. Englewood Cliffs, NJ: Prentice Hall.

Rangan, Kasturi, Lisa Chase, and Sohel Karim. 2015. The truth about CSR. *Harvard Business Review* 93 (1/2): 4049.

Sheehy, Benedict. 2015. Defining CSR: problems and solutions. *Journal of Business Ethics* 131: 625–648.

Vogel, David. 2005. *The market for virtue: the potential and limits of corporate social responsibility*. Washington, DC: The Brookings Institution Press.

**Open Access** This chapter is licensed under the terms of the Creative Commons Attribution 4.0 International License (http://creativecommons.org/licenses/by/4.0/), which permits use, sharing, adaptation, distribution and reproduction in any medium or format, as long as you give appropriate credit to the original author(s) and the source, provide a link to the Creative Commons license and indicate if changes were made.

The images or other third party material in this chapter are included in the chapter's Creative Commons license, unless indicated otherwise in a credit line to the material. If material is not included in the chapter's Creative Commons license and your intended use is not permitted by statutory regulation or exceeds the permitted use, you will need to obtain permission directly from the copyright holder.

# Chapter 11
# Conclusion

This book began with a description of an ethical dilemma: whether an issuer of subprime credit cards should cut in half the credit limits of customers who use their card to pay for marital counseling. The chapters that followed have not suggested what the right answer is, or even whether there is a single "right" answer. Instead, they have described why an organization should take such an issue seriously and how it might go about reaching a considered, responsible decision about it. What have we learned about how an organization should handle the ethical dilemmas that its own use of advanced analytics and AI can create?

Chapter 3 (Risks) helped us to think about ways in which business use of these technologies can harm others. In the subprime credit card scenario, for example, we can see risks to privacy as the card company uses customer purchase information to predict the individual's credit-worthiness—information that the card holders did not know they were revealing. The risk of error also rears its head. Without sufficient attention to data quality and data science (and perhaps even with such attention), the card company will incorrectly classify some card holders. How will this impact those mistakenly deprived of the credit they need? Opacity and procedural unfairness also affect card holders who may not know why the company has reduced cut their credit limit in half and so do not feel empowered to challenge this decision. We also see how advanced analytics changes the balance of power between card issuer and card holder, giving the issuer ever more potent insights that they can use to their advantage. The card company's actions may cause harmful bias if turns out that the proxies (pawn shops, massage parlors, marital counseling) correlate to a protected characteristic. Chapter 3 helps us to see that the card company's actions generate each of these risks.

Chapter 4 (What is Data Ethics Management) suggests that, to address these risks, the credit card company may need to go beyond compliance with the law. No law directly prohibits cutting the credit limit of those who engage in marital counseling. Were the subprime card issuer to forego the use of this insight, it would be doing more than the law required. Chapter 5 (Motivations) goes a step further and suggests that it may be in the company's long-term interests to go beyond compliance in this way. If it becomes public (as, in fact, it did) that the company was penalizing those who went to a marriage counselor, this could harm the company's reputation and make potential card holders leery about dealing with it. The growing regulation of algorithmic decision-making, and the company's need to get ready for it, may also make it wise for the card issuer to consider whether it should find other ways to address the risk of card holder default.

Chapter 6 (Drawing Substantive Lines) concluded that sets of AI ethics principles, while important, can be too broad and internally inconsistent to produce a determinate decision. The subprime credit card case bears this out. Good faith arguments can be made for the beneficence of cutting off the credit of those who go to a marital counselor (it saves them from the pain of default) and for the malevolence of doing so (it will deter people from engaging in marital counseling and so hurt marriages and children). It also shows how principles such as beneficence and justice can conflict with one another since, while it may help borrowers to cut them off when they go to marriage counseling, it hardly seems just to do so. Chapter 6 also discussed the gut-level judgment calls that some organizations use to make decisions about data and AI ethics. In the subprime credit card example, a manager using such an approach might conclude that their grandmother would not approve of cutting the credit of those who go to a marital counselor (public expectations) or that, were the shoe on the other foot, the manager would not want the same policy to be applied to them (the Golden Rule). Such judgment calls may, in fact, keep the company in line with social norms. But they hardly constitute a thoughtful or consistent way of resolving such issues. The subprime credit card issuer should strive to develop more general and prospective policies to guide its actions.

Chapter 7 (Management Structures and Functions) drives home the importance of making a specific person or committee responsible for identifying and managing data ethics issues. The subprime credit card issuer would benefit from this advice. If it fails to spot or handles carelessly the marital counseling issue, that could have an important impact on its goodwill, reputation, and future. It needs to allocate responsibility for managing these critical business issues. It may even want to create a cross-functional data and AI ethics committee to consider these questions from multiple perspectives.

Chapter 8 (Management Processes) describes processes that companies use to spot and resolve their data and AI ethics issues. The use of checklists, consultations with external stakeholders, and other methods for identifying data ethics issues may have sensitized the subprime credit card issuer to concerns about cutting the credit of those who go to a marital counselor. The company will also want to think carefully about its processes for deciding such issues, and who gets the final say.

Chapter 9 (Technical Solutions) identifies key technologies and technical practices that can make an organization's advanced analytics and AI practices fairer, more privacy protective, and more explainable. The subprime credit card issuer would do well to consider, and perhaps adopt, these techniques. It would also benefit from an audit to determine whether the proxies it uses for determining who gets their credit cut have a disparate impact on one or more protected groups. The technical dimension of data ethics management, while not the focus on this book, is clearly essential.

As we have just illustrated, this book can be of practical use to organizations that confront a data or AI ethics issue. But that is not all that it does. The book also seeks to serve as a resource for legislators and regulators who, in designing new laws and policies, should understand how companies are currently managing these issues. Current practice is not the same as best practice. But it is the starting point for legislation and regulation. This book gives lawmakers a sense of the ground on which they are building.

The book also seeks to spark more research on data ethics management. Scholars should not only update our study with more current information; they should also conduct evaluative research to identify which approaches work best, and which do not work very well at all. Defining such best practices and, ultimately, integrating them into standards, codes of practice, and laws, is key to protecting individuals and society from threats that the algorithmic economy generates. If organizations—both those in the private sector as is the focus on this book, and governmental bodies—fail to use responsibly the power that advanced analytics and AI give them, they may lose their social license to operate. Should that happen, we would all miss out on the promise that these technologies hold for better health, education, and many other such social goods. We all have a stake in building strong and effective AI and data ethics management.

**Open Access** This chapter is licensed under the terms of the Creative Commons Attribution 4.0 International License (http://creativecommons.org/licenses/by/4.0/), which permits use, sharing, adaptation, distribution and reproduction in any medium or format, as long as you give appropriate credit to the original author(s) and the source, provide a link to the Creative Commons license and indicate if changes were made.

The images or other third party material in this chapter are included in the chapter's Creative Commons license, unless indicated otherwise in a credit line to the material. If material is not included in the chapter's Creative Commons license and your intended use is not permitted by statutory regulation or exceeds the permitted use, you will need to obtain permission directly from the copyright holder.

**SPRINGER NATURE**

## GPSR Compliance

The European Union's (EU) General Product Safety Regulation (GPSR) is a set of rules that requires consumer products to be safe and our obligations to ensure this.

If you have any concerns about our products, you can contact us on ProductSafety@springernature.com

In case Publisher is established outside the EU, the EU authorized representative is:

Springer Nature Customer Service Center GmbH
Europaplatz 3
69115 Heidelberg, Germany

The manufacturer's authorised representative in the EU is Springer Nature Customer Service Centre GmbH, Europaplatz 3, 69115 Heidelberg, Germany. If you have any concerns regarding our products, please contact ProductSafety@springernature.com

Printed and bound by CPI Group (UK) Ltd, Croydon, CR0 4YY

23/03/2026

02076360-0011